Improving Quality in Education

Improving Quality in Education

Charles Hoy, Colin Bayne-Jardine and Margaret Wood

with an Introduction by Maurice Holt

Falmer Press
Taylor & Francis Group

London and New York

First published 2000
by Falmer Press
11 New Fetter Lane, London EC4P 4EE

Simultaneously published in the USA and Canada
by Falmer Press
Garland Inc., 19 Union Square West, New York, NY 10003

Falmer Press is an imprint of the Taylor & Francis Group

© 2000 Charles Hoy, Colin Bayne-Jardine and Margaret Wood

Typeset in Times by Taylor & Francis Books Ltd
Printed and bound in Great Britain by Biddles Ltd,
Guildford and King's Lynn

All rights reserved. No part of this book may be reprinted or
reproduced or utilized in any form or by any electronic, mechanical, or
other means, now known or hereafter invented, including
photocopying and recording, or in any information storage or retrieval
system, without permission in writing from the publishers.

British Library Cataloguing in Publication Data
A catalogue record for this book is available from the British Library

Library of Congress Cataloging in Publication Data
Hoy, Charles
Improving quality in education
Charles Hoy, Colin Bayne-Jardine & Margaret Wood.
Includes bibliographical references and index.
1. School improvement progress—Great Britain. 2. Educational
change—Great Britain. 3. Educational evaluation—Great Britain.
I. Bayne-Jardine, Colin Charles. II. Wood, Margaret, 1957–.
III. Title.
LB2822.84.G7H69 1999
371.2'00941—dc21 99-28140

0–750–70940–5 pbk
0–750–70941–3 hbk

This book is produced in tribute to all those teachers, headteachers, lecturers and Local Education Authority officers who have endured inspection by an external body. Their experience has not been in vain if this book helps to promote a dialogue about the process of building quality into education. Surely all those involved can begin to work together in partnership to improve upon previous best at every stage of education.

Contents

List of illustrations ix
Note on the text xi

Introduction: The Concept of Quality in Education 1
MAURICE HOLT

1 The Quality Business 10

2 Inspecting It In is Out 27

3 Quality Enhancement Through Development Review 40

4 Development From Within 49

5 Validated Self-Review: Towards a Working Model 60

6 Improving Quality Through a Productive Partnership: A Case Study 75

7 Using Problem Solving for Quality Development: Embedding and Sustaining the Process 117

8 Quality: The Search for the Holy Grail of Organizational Development 134

References 145
Index 151

Illustrations

Tables

1.1	Customers and clients	11
1.2	The application of quality	18
1.3	Formal organizations in education	22
7.1	Categories of function and field within education	123
7.2	Model set of questions to address problems	125
7.3	Problem solving action plan	126
7.4	Decision making	129
7.5	Programmed and non-programmed decisions	130

Figures

2.1	Quality development and quality concerns	35
2.2	Balanced concern for educational development	36
3.1	Mentoring roles	45
4.1	The dynamic process of learning	51
4.2	Focus for school development	52
7.1	Problem solving paradigm	126
7.2	Ditch jumping	128
7.3	Solution finding	128
8.1	Staff development and training	136

Note on the text

The terminology used throughout this book follows United States practice by referring to the school as a generic entity, whether it be a primary, elementary or secondary school, further education college or higher education institution.

Dr Charles Hoy
Dr Colin Bayne-Jardine
Dr Margaret Wood
University of Manchester
January 1999

Introduction
The Concept of Quality in Education

Maurice Holt

Until the early 1990s, the pursuit of quality in schools was implicit in such activities as curriculum development, rather than explicit in programmes for school improvement. I remember, though, that I first heard the Q-word when I visited an English comprehensive school in 1982 to learn about a curriculum review that had been launched by the new principal. He told me that he was hoping the staff committee would come up with a 'quality product'. From his careful preparation and seriousness of purpose, I took it he meant a document that would, in important ways, be good for the school and its students. But to use 'quality' in this way seemed to have interesting implications, while the term 'product' struck me as more appropriate to business than education.

But then, 1982 was the year when *In Search of Excellence: Lessons from America's Best-Run Companies* was published (Peters and Waterman, 1982). Tom Peters and Robert Waterman, you will recall, examined sixty-two successful companies and identified eight characteristics common to them all. They suggested that the rational model of scientific management had little to do with the running of successful companies. They made a passing reference to quality control, but quality, as we have come to know it, is not part of their argument. The concept of quality as a management doctrine in the US was only just beginning to emerge within the car industry.

By the early 1980s, competition from Japan had generated a desperate financial crisis at the Ford Motor Company – ironically so, since Ford management was dominated by the 'bean counters', accountants dedicated to reducing costs and tightening budgets. The Japanese automakers had taken a different path in the post-war years, following the advice of the American management thinker Edwards Deming, and were now exporting cars that Americans found to be more reliable and more affordable than the home-grown product. In 1981, as the company faced financial ruin, Ford finally invited Deming to Detroit and began a mammoth rethink, based on his philosophy of the management of quality (Gabor, 1990). The success of this turnaround operation is beyond dispute: in 1997, Ford took the lead in

Introduction

the American market, and in the UK Ford cars now consistently emerge at the top of consumer ratings.

Deming's ideas can be simply expressed but easily misunderstood. Although they evolved within a business context, they amount to a philosophy of moral action that regards organizations as systems subject to variation (Holt, 1993). They therefore address a concept of quality – of what it is good to do – that can be applied to non-profit activities such as public education.

During the 1990s, as the notion of managing quality has become more formalized in business applications, so several attempts have been made to transfer Deming's ideas – and those of other quality gurus – to educational settings. But in the rush to do so, slogans have often displaced substance and first principles have been overlooked. For example, Deming attaches great importance, in business settings, to addressing the present and future needs of the customer. This has led to speculation by various education writers, debating whether the pupil can be both customer and product, and whether the customer is the parent or the taxpayer. Asked about this in some of his seminars, Deming (1993) gave a characteristic reply:

> We go overboard on words. Society should be the beneficiary. We don't have customers in education. Don't forget your horse sense.

(This, by the way, should not be confused with common sense, which can be very misleading: 'Common sense tells us that the earth is flat.')

This brief introduction is intended to serve two purposes: to outline the history of quality as a management strategy; and to indicate Deming's role as a major player. From this perspective, I turn now to the meaning we might attribute to quality in education, and to the ways in which it might be promoted or undermined.

There need be no great mystery about what we mean by quality. In general terms, if we say that an article or activity has the attribute of quality, then it exhibits some kind of excellence or distinction that makes it desirable and beneficial. As Deming puts it, 'A product or service possesses quality if it helps somebody and enjoys a good and sustainable market' (Deming, 1994). Schooling, for example, benefits society by helping the student, in Michael Oakeshott's phrase, to make something of himself.

A few examples will help clarify these points. An interesting case is the much-esteemed P51 Mustang fighter that first came into service with the Royal Air Force during 1943. The design and prototype were produced in six months by the North American Corporation, in response to an urgent request from the British, and made use of advanced aerodynamic data obtained from the US National Advisory Committee for Aeronautics even though the US Air Force initially had little interest in the project. Conceived quickly, and probably without detailed specifications, the circumstances permitted a good deal of initiative. The design team combined a firm grasp of theory (its laminar-flow wing was a new departure) with a shrewd understanding of practical engineering, and the Mustang proved to be capable of sustained technical development in a variety of roles and theatres of war. The Mustang possessed quality, because quality had been built into its conception and execution.

The Sony Walkman, first introduced in 1979, has become a popular everyday convenience. From the beginning it worked well, and its imitators testify to its originality. It was the result not of market research or focus groups, nor of the endless evaluation of existing products, but of the innovative style of its manufacturers, whose idea of product development is 'to lead the market with new products', not to ask consumers what kind of products they want (Collins and Porras, 1997). In Deming's terms, it helps people and it enjoys a good market.

Think next of an Impressionist painting by an admired artist of that school. We notice the shimmering sky, the delicate play of light, the subtle treatment of the rippling water – but above all we respond to a certain inimitable character, a feeling for atmosphere and mood, that the painting radiates as a whole. The painting has a unique quality. We could analyse its elements, even suggest the procedures followed by the artist; but its quality is innate and inimitable, and springs from the ideas that gave it birth.

In each case, quality is inherent in the product – indeed, quality is itself a product, and not a process. To suppose otherwise is to misunderstand the nature of quality. Quality results from the system that produced it, and is an attribute of that system as much as of the product itself: of its processes, its people, the way they work together. Quality cannot be defined as a particular procedure, nor can we guarantee quality simply by controlling each stage in the process. Quality stems from the way in which the product takes shape as it moves through the system; it resists hierarchy and eludes determinism.

For these reasons, Deming greatly disliked the term 'total quality management'. It implies that all you have to do is collect data at each stage, optimize it and wait for the desired products to emerge as the sequence proceeds. But ends and means interact: the action is organic and complex, not procedural and linear. Painting by numbers cannot reproduce a Monet. Quality certainly involves a desire for improvement, but improvement alone is not enough. Innovation is needed, as the Sony Walkman demonstrates. So also is a synthesis of theory and practice, as in the case of the Mustang fighter.

The notion of 'quality assurance' is equally threadbare. The idea here is to define benchmarks or specified performance at particular stages, and assume that if these are observed, quality will be inherent. In Deming's view, a fatal move in any organization is the appointment of a 'Director of Quality'. Immediately, responsibility for improvement and innovation is transferred from the entire system – the suppliers, designers, manufacturers, consumers – to a nebulous job specification.

Turning to quality in school systems, the first step is to consider what the 'product' might be that is to possess quality. I shall suppose that education is concerned with the development of the minds of pupils; schools produce educated persons who, by virtue of their schooling, make their way in society to their own and society's benefit. So far, so good; but we encounter a difficulty immediately. How are these benefits to be construed? Is our aim to be the pursuit of happiness? The creation of wealth through capitalism? The religious life, made manifest? Our concept of quality is dependent on which we choose.

In any society, its sense of purpose will change from time to time. The America of the 1990s focuses on success in the global economy; in the 1960s, human rights and personal freedom were prominent. Britain has experienced a similar sea-change in its aspirations, and its current obsessions in education address the material rather than the numinous: schools must show what the pupils 'know and can do', and will be held accountable in those terms. So attainment targets are specified and compliance is demanded; thus will pupils be prepared for the world of business.

The danger, on the other hand, is that pupils schooled in this way might turn out to be better equipped for yesterday's business than tomorrow's. Sony, Ford, Boeing and other farseeing companies need people with the imagination to fly free from the world of facts and figures and create, not replicate. Quality depends on an intelligent, questioning workforce at every level. And these are precisely the propensities that do not yield to numerical tests and targets – indeed, they are stifled by them.

The fact is, though, that in the minds of most legislators and in the pages of the tabloid press, quality is linked with accountability: if a school comes out well on tests, grades and targets, it must possess quality. So the quest for quality becomes the imposition of benchmarks, the incorporation of 'best practice' out of context and the relentless pursuit of management objectives defined as targets and results. But a school may do well on such measures, simply because it is teaching to the test. The curriculum may be impoverished, yet still satisfy the demands of accountability. According to Winch (1996), the accountable school may lack quality.

Quality cannot be a matter of fulfilling performance targets. There is no point in setting targets without knowing how to meet them. And if we knew how to meet them, we would already have fulfilled them. Managing the process by working backwards from targets, objectives or results is, as Deming puts it, 'like driving by looking in the rearview mirror'. All these strategies stem from the old, top-down, line-management model, identified as a failure by Peters and Waterman all those years ago. Yet they dominate the thinking of national policymakers, particularly in the UK, where these errors are compounded by a seriously misconceived system of inspection.

Introduction

The capacity of a system to generate quality cannot be determined by numerical measures. As Deming often remarked, 'The most important figures needed for the management of any organisation are unknown and unknowable' (Neave, 1990). In the case of educational assessment, the uncertainties are legion. To suppose that the intellectual worth of a student can be summarized by an array of numbers is an extraordinary notion in itself, and particularly so when the numbers are of dubious value, and when the means of getting them have such a destructive effect on the educational encounter. For a detailed account of these matters, which space prevents here, I refer the reader to recent studies by both Andrew Davis and Alfie Kohn. Alfie Kohn's two books (Kohn, 1992 and 1993) offer detailed refutations of the view that sticks, carrots and competition promote learning; while Davis (1998) provides a scholarly account of why educational assessment is fundamentally flawed.

Some researchers have attempted to escape from this dilemma by advocating the concept of school effectiveness. Various indicators are developed, usually by identifying schools deemed to be 'successful', using black-box research techniques measuring input and output characteristics and statistical analysis that 'factors out' differences. It is now widely acknowledged that most 'effective' schools display five or six characteristics which most of us could write down without much thought on the back of an envelope.

But it is one thing to identify such traits; quite another to discover how to instil them. And in any case, as Neil Postman has remarked, we may be able to make the trains run on time (which is what effective school research is all about); but suppose they are running to the wrong place (Postman, 1996)? The difficulty is with the word 'effective'. High-rise apartment blocks were an effective way of housing urban populations in the 1960s, but they soon turned out to be an expensive mistake. As Bill Reid has argued, the term 'effective' is devoid of moral content, and it is an inappropriate concept to apply to the moral activity of schooling (Reid, 1997).

How, then, should we determine what constitutes an educated person? We must be clear that, in the public sector, this is a political question: educational theory is irrelevant if our recommendation carries no conviction with parents and other stakeholders, not least the students themselves. For enlightenment, I therefore turn to the 1998 *Phi Delta Kappa/Gallup poll of the public's attitudes toward the public schools* (Rose and Gallup, 1998). Respondents were offered six indicators of school effectiveness and asked to state the importance of each. Top of the list came 'The percentage of students who graduate from high school', with 82 per cent agreeing that this was 'very important'. Bottom came 'Scores that students receive on standardized tests', with a 50 per cent rating. This result is encouraging to those of us who believe that parents value the entire effect of a particular school, because that is what the notion of graduation is about. It also confirms that parents are loath to rely too much on tests; they trust school-based

Introduction

judgment of a student's capacity rather than decontextualized external assessment.

I pause for a moment at this point to mention that the HMI (Her Majesty's Inspector) system of inspection, so thoughtlessly destroyed by the Conservative government a few years ago, was intended to offer a view of the entire effect of a school. It was not an inspection of teachers, nor of pupils: it was an informed judgment by a team of able professionals on a complex institution – indeed, it was an attempt to determine its quality. The virtues of the approach have been recognized by New York State (which is establishing a similar system), and a study of the pre-Thatcher Inspectorate would be helpful in any enquiry into strategies for promoting school quality.

I am suggesting, then, that at some point in the future, when current fashion gives way to a more spacious, more generous concept of curriculum and assessment, policymakers would do well to notice that the public may have a more liberal view of the function of schooling and its evaluation than it has been given credit for. A school-designed, broad-based curriculum offering a variety of learning and assessment strategies, in a context of autonomy within a local authority system, would give freedom to innovate, enhance pupil engagement and promote quality.

A more flexible approach to assessment is essential if accountability and quality are to be reconciled. Any industrial process is subject to variation from many sources – raw materials, equipment wear, climatic change – and controlling it, as Deming recognized, is vital in sustaining quality. In education, variation among students must assuredly be taken into account as something not to be eliminated but to be celebrated. The apparatus of a defined national or state curriculum, geared to achievement testing, is in effect a denial of variation. Again, this is a political issue as much as a technical one, and it will need political courage to grasp it when the climate is right.

By the same token, a school curriculum needs to be exactly that – a curriculum that works for *this* school, with *these* parents and teachers, and adapted for *these* pupils. School districts and local education authorities need the authority and security to be able to divest themselves of much of their power, and work out ways in which school autonomy can be reconciled with the modalities of the system as a whole.

In this regard, local authority schemes to foster in schools practices that promote quality are to be welcomed, providing the issue of assessment is squarely faced. Assessment and evaluation certainly constitute an element in any system dedicated to quality, but they should not dominate it, particularly in education. In the first place, formal, summative assessment is unreliable and generates a climate of competition. Infinitely more desirable, from the point of view of the learning encounter, is informal, formative teacher-based assessment intrinsic to the teaching process. But these benefits are seriously attenuated once teacher-based assessment is formalized and

Introduction

becomes extrinsic to the learning encounter. Systems of self-assessment suffer from this difficulty, and there is the danger that with so much soul-searching and over-thinking, improvement can turn into what Deming calls 'tampering' – changing the process for the sake of it. Moreover, all this assessment consumes nervous energy and time better spent teaching.

Bear in mind, too, that there are few more boring things to do in school than assess pupils in a formal way. It is a tiresome raking over of old bones, casting gloom on everyone it touches. It is quite wrong to suppose that we can only manage what we can measure; on the contrary, what we can measure is often not worth managing. And a climate of assessing and evaluating is not conducive to innovation: it fosters a bank manager's view of intellectual endeavour. The safest rule for all forms of extrinsic assessment – assessment detached from the learning encounter itself – is to regard it as a necessary evil, and keep it to the minimum required by the accounting body. And the closer accountability moves to the individual school and its stakeholders, the smaller that minimum becomes.

When Boeing decided to go ahead and build the 747 jumbo jet, it was 'as much because of its self-identity as because of its desire for profits – because it believed it should be on the leading edge of air transportation'. Some studies had been carried out on the projected return on investment, but the results were so inconclusive they were ignored (Collins and Porras, 1997). The 'self-identity' of the school is important, too; if a school decides, for example, to build a humanities programme linking history, geography and English, and can carry with it the support of parents and the local authority, it makes sense to do so since the putative 'return on investment' is a prize worth going for.

I have drawn freely upon examples from the world of business in discussing the management of quality, but I would resist the suggestion that education is in any sense a business. Helping the young discover their capacities is an altogether more enthralling and, indeed, more responsible undertaking than designing the world's first transistor radio. Any analogy between the two activities must be drawn with the greatest care. The curriculum is not a collection of defined activities and programmes, to be delivered by teacher-operations in accordance with government stipulations and weighed as if it were a commodity. The school curriculum is a remarkably complex set of intentions and interactions, full of intangibles and truly assessable in its effects only in years to come.

At the same time, it will be clear from the examples I have given that the most progressive and idealistic companies would align themselves much more with the latter description of the school curriculum than with my account of the 'delivery system' view of education. The surprising thing is that, although these are companies which do not put a premium on making profits, they often turn out to be successful in that regard as well. Nothing but good can come from examining other enterprises that share with schools

Introduction

certain fundamentals: a sense of purpose, the management of talented professionals, a concern for working in teams while respecting individuals, a reluctance to make premature judgments for improvement and a readiness to innovate.

I therefore conclude by mentioning a recent American study of 'visionary companies' by Jim Collins and Jerry Porras which both updates the 1982 work of Peters and Waterman and uses a much more rigorous research base (Collins and Porras, 1997). *Built to Last* is not specifically about quality – the word does not appear in the index – but it might well have been. (In fact, the term 'quality' has become so debased during the 1990s that using it can sometimes foster misunderstanding.) The book examines the work of eighteen companies that it identifies as 'premier institutions...in their industries, widely admired by their peers and having a long track record of making a significant impact on the world around them'. For each such visionary company, a comparison company is named that does not 'quite match up to the overall stature' of its peer. Boeing, for example, is compared with McDonnell Douglas, Ford with General Motors.

The study comes up with some interesting conclusions about the really durable, adaptable organizations. They do not require charismatic leaders; they do not exist primarily to maximize profits; their ideologies vary; and they maintain their core values while displaying 'a powerful drive for progress'. Neither do they play it safe – they commit to audacious goals, and 'make some of their best moves by experimentation, trial and error, opportunism, and...accident'. They continually seek to improve what they do, focusing on beating themselves rather than their competitors. And they avoid simple dualities of the 'we can do this or that, but not both' variety. They believe you can have your cake *and* eat it.

All of these observations have some relevance to schools that wish to build good reputations and do the best for their students in good times and bad. It is helpful to have headteachers who listen and respond, rather than use the school as an instrument for magnifying their own personalities. Rather than maximize exam results – a reasonable analogue of profits – good schools focus on curriculum design and the organization of learning, knowing that, if these are right, the results will follow. And such schools are not all alike; there are many ideologies that work, and it is folly to suppose that good practice can be transferred from one school to another.

The emphasis on 'core values', and on the innate life of the school or company as an institution, reminds one of the view of Alasdair MacIntyre (1982) that institutions are characterized by a 'practice':

> A coherent and complex form of socially established cooperative human activity through which goods internal to that form of activity are realised...with the result that human powers to achieve excellence...are systematically extended.

This describes pretty well what Collins and Porras have identified in their visionary companies, and it might equally well describe the ferment of ideas, conflicts and actions in a school with the attribute of quality. MacIntyre's account is a valuable formal reminder of the 'internal goods' through which quality is generated. Given that kind of institutional practice, it is easy to see how bold new projects can be visualized and enacted.

It is good to be reminded, too, that competing with oneself is as salutary for institutions as it is for individuals. Not the least objection to the 'league tables' that list schools in rank order of exam results is their tendency to promote meaningless competition, dissipating energies and undermining cooperation. And the finding that you can have your cake and eat it is particularly important at a time when the arts are squeezed out of the curriculum because so much time is prescribed for core subjects. The truth is that any school can design a curriculum that includes science *and* drama; that uses mixed-ability teaching *and* gets good exam results; that can satisfy the demands of accountability and encourage pupils to criticise, invent and think for themselves.

It is, of course, the case that much of what I have outlined here is, at present, seriously circumscribed in the US by the America 2000 programme, with its goals and assessments; and even more so in the UK by the National Curriculum and its attendant apparatus of benchmarks, targets and teacher-proof programmes. One of the more dismaying events of the last ten years was perhaps the welcome given by the academic establishment in the UK to the National Curriculum – a straitjacket for eliminating quality and fostering mediocrity. To their credit, Americans are infinitely more suspicious of attempts to impose uniformity on their schools. There is a case for considering national guidelines, locally interpreted, but not for stipulative outcomes so detailed and all-encompassing that they grossly extend the power of central government, such that any deviation technically breaks the law of the land.

But times change, and nothing goes on for ever. Ideas circulate, books like this one get written, and schools, mercifully, are full of optimists. They can also be inventive; some have found ways of having the National Curriculum cake and eating it too. Quality is never an impossible dream.

1 The Quality Business

> Quality in education is somewhat problematical: like beauty, it lies in the eye – or rather the mind – of the beholder
>
> (Cliff, Nuttall and McCormick, 1987)

We suggest that some of the confusion surrounding the issue of quality in education arises because the assessment of three separate interest groups of purchasers is being convoluted and compressed into one single measure. This overlooks the separate interests of three very distinct groups of people – those who pay for the process, those who are engaged in receiving the process and those who benefit from the output from the process of education. In addition it is not simply a question of quality of what, for whom and to which purposes, since even the education service differs little from other more mundane purchases that we, as individuals or groups, may make during our lives. There is a very basic difference between customers and clients in any centrally provided service such as education. In education, there is no simple single transaction between purchaser and provider.

Customers and Clients

If we say that those who take away the goods or buy the services at a shop are the 'customers', then in most cases they will have paid for those goods themselves. In the case of education, on the other hand, there is a group of 'clients' who have paid for those goods indirectly, through their taxes. They are represented at both 'ends' of the process, while the students are seen in the middle.

This leads us to a working definition of Quality in Education:

> Quality in Education is an evaluation of the process of educating which enhances the need to achieve and develop the talents of the customers of the process, and at the same time meets the accountability standards set by the clients who pay for the process or the outputs from the process of educating.

The Quality Business

The customer and the client, therefore, both have an equally valid interest in the quality of the goods. The students or their parental representatives may have a direct interest in the quality of the education provision, but equally the Local Education Authorities (LEAs) and the Department for Education and Employment (DfEE) have a direct interest also. These interests are of two kinds. The student has sat at the feet of the teacher and invested time and effort in trying to learn. The taxpayers' representatives, assisted by their officers, are involved in an assessment of the cost of the process of educating the students and so too are the ultimate beneficiaries of the process of educating – the employers.

Considering the different interests of each group, and remembering that the North American usage of the word 'school' covers all types of educational institutions from primary or elementary schools, middle or high schools, we set out a list of customers and clients in Table 1.1.

The three basic definitions of quality – quality assurance, contract conformance and customer driven – add a further dimension to our working definition. Quality assurance refers to the determination of standards by an expert body such as the Office For Standards in Education (OFSTED), while contract conformance refers to the situation in which the quality standard has been negotiated during the formation of the contract. Special needs provision would fall within this form of quality. The third definition, customer-driven quality, relates clearly to the expectations and requirements of the customer, and we have already suggested that there is a need to clarify the groups included within that term (Murgatroyd and Morgan, 1993).

There can be no doubt that both customer and client have become more sophisticated in their demands upon the products and services provided by

Table 1.1 Customers and clients

'Customers' – Students and employers	'Clients' – Local Education Authorities, central government
Interested in:	*Interested in*:
Actual learning and teaching they receive from their teachers	Quality of resources (professional competence; buildings and materials) at local and central levels equally
Need for some verification processes for seeing that the service is up to standards set by customers before they pay for the service?	Need for some verification processes for seeing that the service is up to standards set by clients before they pay for the service?
Value for money: time and effort in exams taken by the students	Assessment of the material curriculum, the institutional provisions (accreditation), and of the professional competence of the teachers delivering the service (test their abilities – at start, and regularly throughout their careers)

educational organizations. Murgatroyd and Morgan (1993) argue convincingly that the balance needs to be shifted from quality assurance activity towards customer driven and contract performance activity. In simple terms, the resources used to power the OFSTED machine should be shifted to the organizations involved in teaching and learning, with the requirement that they set up systems for consulting the internal customer. The major difficulty over such a shift from quality assurance is the need to accept the loss of a certain degree of central control.

What is Quality?

Quality in education is clearly linked to purpose. A variety of assumptions and values underpins perceptions of the purpose of education in a democracy. Following a Jeffersonian philosophy, we believe in the vital importance of unlocking the potential of all citizens. Education is to do with learning, rather than with social control and advantage.

The pursuit of the nature of quality within the definition is like peeling the skins off an onion. Indeed, at times tears of frustration pour down the enquirer's cheeks as the definition is elusive. We believe that quality is dependent upon the particular context in which it is to be applied. It is specific to an arena. Quality is essentially part of the learning process, a learning process that is the purpose of an educational organisation.

In the impressive Quality Development Resource Pack produced by Birmingham City Council (1992), Tim Brighouse writes of 'the strong local dialect of a process which is vital to school improvements'. The written guidance has to be given a voice that draws people into a professional dialogue and involves them in the process. By using a dialect and language that appeals, the process of quality development becomes part of the warp and weft of education. In this way, improving quality in education covers the process of assuring continued enhancement of the service to meet ever-exacting expectations from increasingly discerning client groups. Like religious principles there is a basis of sincere beliefs for which there is neither empirical evidence nor rational foundation.

There is much evidence regarding the factors that make for effective schools (Sammons et al., 1995). However, as Maurice Holt has pointed out in the Introduction to this volume, it is one thing to analyse the factors that are present in an effective school, but quite another to instil them elsewhere. Schools are learning organizations, and as we peel off the onion layers of quality we are faced with the question of how schools can be supported in their provision of quality education.

In *Success Against the Odds* (1996) Margaret Maden and Josh Hillman tease out the lessons from eleven case studies of successful schools in disadvantaged areas. They point out that every school has the opportunity to succeed against the odds. They go on to say:

Improvement is achieved by the whole school: by the teachers, but also by the pupils; by all the staff, not only the teachers; and by the parents and the wider community.

Quality does not come 'gift-wrapped'; rather, it needs consistent involvement by all in the process of developing pupils' learning.

Quality can be seen in today's consumer oriented society as being to do with fulfilling the expectations of consumers. 'Quality', 'value' and 'choice' are part of the consumerist dogma in relation to goods and services. Quality has thus become one of the watchwords of the consumer's creed, and quality standards are enshrined in consumer charters: charters for parents, patients, job seekers and so on. The language of quality is redolent with the terminology of consumerism and co-terminous with the concepts of 'fitness for purpose' and 'value for money'. Measures of quality in terms of National Health Service care, for example, might include length of waiting lists for patients and mortality rates at hospitals. The assumption here is that there are indicators by which quality can be judged – how many trains run on time? How many children gain more than five A–C grades in the General Certificate of Secondary Education? Other measures which may be used as yardsticks by which to make a judgment about the quality of education can include: attendance figures; staying-on rates; exclusion figures; qualifications of teaching staff; staff absentee rates; pupil:teacher ratios; class sizes.

Perceptions of quality have important implications for schools. Each stakeholder may have his/her own 'quality standard' against which to arrive at a judgment. Parents, children, governors, industry and business, the government may each have a different perspective. Is quality to be judged, for example, by the extent to which government targets for literacy or numeracy have been met? Are Charter Marks and Investor In People status telling us something about quality? Is quality therefore to do with performance against externally set standards? As Maurice Holt has pointed out, quality as defined by Deming is inherent in a product rather than an end in itself.

There are many approaches to quality: quality control, quality assurance, quality enhancement, quality development/quality improvement and total quality management (TQM). At one end of such a spectrum, quality is more to do with compliance with a product specification. At the other end it is to do with empowerment and self-determination.

Quality can be graded 'low' or 'high', and in this book on improving the quality of education we address what we believe to be the highest quality. In other words, the best practice and how it can be enhanced. In this sense we are using 'quality' as both a noun and an adjective: 'quality' understood as high quality and excellence; and the qualities of the improvement process in education whereby a high degree of excellence is achieved.

We are also writing about quality within a value framework through which we see the best or highest quality as an entitlement for all. Quality and equality are linked together in this way, and we believe that improving quality in education must reduce the 'quality gap' which exists for those who may experience inequality due to race, social class, residence, religious belief or the like. *Success Against the Odds* (Maden and Hillman, 1996) outlines the ways in which quality processes can overcome the obstacles to provide quality learning for pupils in disadvantaged areas. The 'quality gap' is merely widened by low expectations. To say 'Well, what can you expect from these children?' makes the underachievers doubly disadvantaged as opposed to being empowered.

Comparative judgments are made about quality: for example, unfavourable comparisons between schools in the United Kingdom and Pacific Rim schools. Part of the current context for quality is 'zero tolerance' – poorest quality will not, therefore, be countenanced. One of the policy principles of a recent government White Paper, *Excellence in schools* (DfEE, 1997a) states that 'There will be zero tolerance of under-performance':

> Our aim is excellence for everyone. If this is to be more than rhetoric, then persistent failure must be eradicated. Hence our commitment to zero tolerance of under-performance. We shall seize every opportunity to recognize and celebrate success in the education service, and we shall put in place policies which seek to avoid failure. But where failure occurs, we shall tackle it head on. Schools which have been found to be failing will have to improve, make a fresh start, or close. The principle of zero tolerance will also apply to local education authorities. Our policy will be driven by our recognition that children only get one chance. We intend to create an education service in which every school is either excellent, improving or both.
>
> (DfEE, 1997a, *Excellence in schools*, p. 12)

The other side of this is the recognition of outstanding quality, for example 'Beacon Schools' to act as 'guiding lights', beacons of quality and excellence. The Teacher Training Agency's framework of national professional standards for newly qualified teachers and serving teachers at different stages as they progress in their careers can be seen as a way of building quality improvements into the profession. It is vital to remember that all such judgments are value judgments.

Accountability as a stimulus to quality improvement can be seen in the very public ways in which superior quality is afforded pre-eminence and extolled, while poor quality, in the sense of failure to meet expectations of adequate standards, is publicly known and closely scrutinized and monitored. In this way quality is part of the process within an organization while

The Quality Business

it has to meet the expectations of client groups outside the organization. Both customers and clients are taking part in the definition of quality education. In many ways, in fact, this strengthens the role of quality education.

The school mission statement encapsulates the core purposes and values of the school, and the extent to which this is fulfilled says something about the school and the measure of success achieved. But there are dangers inherent in assessing quality solely in terms of the extent to which a school can demonstrate that it is meeting its own criteria for success – an external perspective is needed too. This will guard against insularity and introspection, and contextualize the work of the school within a broader framework of national and local expectations. This brings us to the idea of 'partnerships for quality'. The school has a number of partners for quality development – three important ones are the Department for Education and Employment (DfEE), the Local Education Authority (LEA), and the Office for Standards in Education (OFSTED). Each of these can bring an external validation of the work of the school and can challenge the school to improve on current performance in order to achieve ever-higher levels of quality. Ambitious and challenging targets set at national and local levels are intended as incentives in the drive for higher rates of success and enhanced quality of teaching and learning which must lie at the heart of the core mission for every school.

A good leader inspires commitment to the core purposes of the organization – this is one of the qualities of leadership that is vital. When examining the quality of education in schools we must acknowledge the central role of the leader and his/her ability to lend strategic direction. Without this capability, a school is likely to be tossed and turned by each tide of educational change. It may be thrown from its direction and path as it responds to the tumultuous demands and forces which seek to act upon it. In adopting a responsive stance, its sense of direction can become confused; development may thus be hastily accomplished and performed in random and haphazard ways. Without vision, direction is lost and quality is sacrificed.

Quality is often defined in terms of outcomes to match a customer's satisfaction. This gives rise to the definition of quality as the extent to which the outcomes meet the customer's requirements. Competence-based quality results need to be supported by a capability to deliver the service on the part of everyone involved. The inevitable outcome for this system is to reward those who can deliver a quality product, and to train those who cannot.

Quality can also be defined by means of identifying longer-term aims which help to define medium-term goals and lead to the immediate short-term objectives. By closely specifying objectives and striving to achieve them, we find ourselves led towards the achievement of related goals in pursuit of the ultimate aims. In the whole process, the key to the prison of our depression over quality issues is the decision to value ourselves, to define our own mission statement, to have a vision and be demanding, to have an agenda and be insistent, to know where we are going, and why. A 'Quality Education' comes from making things happen, not letting things happen to you. There are no secrets to success in quality enhancement, so looking for them is a waste of time. Success is the result of perfecting the process, hard work and learning from failure. We trust that in this book we have set out our means to that end, the search for the holy grail of continued professional development towards the aim of enhanced quality in education. One major obstacle in the way of attempts to build quality into the learning process is the desire to control education from outside schools, colleges and universities.

The Control of the Process

The control of education is and always has been of fundamental importance to both local and central government. Local government is concerned because the schooling of the children of any community will have immediate implications for the health and wealth of that community. The central government likewise is concerned for the national interest to ensure a continuance of the developments in health, welfare, social and economic terms of the nation state. Therein lies the dichotomy. Who ought to have the over-riding control, the ultimate power in terms of what is taught, how it is delivered and by whom, and what mechanisms should be involved in its monitoring, evaluation and review? In addition, how should the learners be managed?

Even more important are the teachers and lecturers in the school or college, whose task is to encourage learning in their students. Who is to control their input, who is to determine their expertise, their quality and where improvement should start? Such fundamental interests are likely to clash in cases where there is no overarching consensus as to the immediate, medium- and longer-term objectives of schooling, or where there is rapid change in the realization of objectives. This section looks at the ways of analysing this complex interaction, primarily from the perspective of the Local Education Authority and the schools, though with allowances for other interested power centres present in the debate over the allocation of control.

Education is in an age of transition. Changes have taken place in the control of education at all levels over the past few years, starting with the Education Acts of 1986 and 1988. The perception of all that is undertaken in education is increasingly related to cash equivalent terms. The Audit Commission for Local Authorities in England and Wales stated in its Summary (1989):

To discharge their own educational responsibilities, Local Education Authorities (LEAs) need assurance, independent of institutional management, that education of a satisfactory quality is being provided. That assurance can come, only as a result of professional monitoring, including direct observation (inspection). Measures to secure improvement also require a detached professional input (advice).

If this concept is compared to that of the Office For Standards in Education (OFSTED) set out in 'Planning Improvement: Schools' Post Inspection Action Plans' (1995), two things emerge. The words under the OFSTED logo, 'Improvement through inspection', contradict the above Audit Commission definition, and a major responsibility of LEAs, namely for the quality of education, is undermined.

Under the inspection proposals from OFSTED of 15 July 1997 there was a premium on teacher adaptability and an ability to be all things to all people. The need currently appears to be for teachers to be able to convince the inspectors how well they have managed their teaching. The major evidence base is the level of the examination and test results. League tables simply reinforce this.

There are surprising differences between the three external assessment processes currently applied to schools, further education colleges and universities. School inspection through OFSTED – now even more finely targeted – is aimed at the *individual* classroom teacher's competence, whereas the Higher Education Funding Council's (HEFC) Quality Assessment is directed to the learning achieved by the students in a particular *department* of a university, while the Further Education Funding Council (FEFC) assesses and grades the *whole college* as a single entity. At present there is no body charged with the process of assessing the application of these functions overall to the education system in England and Wales.

A model to decipher the individual applications to the various sectors of education in this country is offered in Table 1.2.

Rewriting the OFSTED 'Framework for the Inspection of Schools'(1998; DfEE, 1997c) documents in a positive and supportive light – rather than focusing on failure and failing schools – might just possibly provide a framework for a satisfactory school. Yet within any such framework there is a further factor to consider. Gunnar Myrdal's higher and lower valuations (Myrdal, 1944) need to be borne in mind in relation to the issues of quality, and particularly to inspection report statements. Higher valuations are those that no-one opposes, those that are always agreed to in questionnaires and interviews – statements that consistently appeal to the norms and mores of almost all people involved in an activity. Lower valuations are the basis upon which people act – the ways they behave. These, Myrdal believed, were at odds with their own stated standards of action. The case studies in

The Quality Business

Table 1.2 The application of quality

Quality applications focus	The individual	The class or subject	The school, college or university	Funding body
Quality assessment mechanisms				
Internal assessment	Staff appraisal	Departmental development review	Whole school	Political?\discussions
	Peer review			
External Assessment	OFSTED inspection	HEFC inspection	FEFC inspection	Annual reports?
The self-developing school or department	Mentoring	Working party and or paired review group	'Quality Committee'	Quality Review Committee?
Impact affects:	Self-esteem	Departmental climate	College status	Political credibility
Funding changes:	Nil	Potentially severe	Potentially severe	

Chapter 6 demonstrate the crucial importance of teacher involvement in quality assessments.

Another layer can be peeled from the onion of quality at this stage. If quality is part of the process, and we are seeking high quality, then those involved in the process must be motivated to give their best. Improvement may be down to an individual's need to achieve, in terms described by McClelland (1961). This motivation is set within a context that governments often change, as Beeby (1966 and 1967) suggested. Policy is, in some measure, determined by the ways and means chosen. This particular interaction has not entered into the OFSTED approach to inspection, nor has an understanding of the complexity of the process of learning been acknowledged.

While we may not be so ready to accept Beeby's views on the development of quality in school systems now compared to the heady days of the 1960s, there is probably still more than a grain of truth in his assertions (Beeby, 1966) – if taken as guides to our own evaluation of quality in education:

There are various stages of growth through which all school systems must pass; although a system may be helped to speed up its progress, it cannot leapfrog a stage or portion of a stage because its position on a scale of development is determined by two factors: the level of general education of the teachers, and the amount of training they have had.

Reversing the OFSTED-failing schools criteria (DfEE, 1995a) might provide a better framework for improving quality. The 'Quality' school would look like this in terms of education standards to be achieved:

1. Satisfactory attainment and progress in the subjects of the curriculum by the majority of pupils. This will be evident in examination assessment and other accredited results.
2. Absence of disruptive behaviour, discipline problems or exclusions.
3. No incidents of racial tension or harassment.
4. Satisfactory attendance by a substantial proportion of pupils, and by particular groups of pupils, together with low levels of truancy.

The quality of education provided would also include:

1. A high proportion of satisfactory teaching, including high expectation of pupils.
2. Full implementation of the National Curriculum.
3. Very good provision for pupils' spiritual, moral, social and cultural development.
4. No pupils at physical or emotional risk from other pupils or adults in the school.
5. No abrasive and confrontational relationships between staff and pupils.

The management and efficiency of the school would be characterized by:

1. Effective headteacher, senior management and governors.
2. Full confidence in the headteacher by the staff, parents and governors.
3. Commitment and belief in all staff, low levels of staff turnover and absence.
4. Good management and efficient use of resources, including finance, available to the school.
5. Good value for money provided by the school.

What is being looked for is evidence of a high proportion of satisfactory teaching, fully implementing the National Curriculum, with satisfactory provision for the students' spiritual, moral, social and cultural development; not a deficiency-based OFSTED model, but rather an achievement oriented identity, for both the individuals and the institutions concerned. Teachers having a high expectation of their students' performance are likely to do a better job than those who are being criticized as failing.

Naturally, changes in the attitudes of many individuals will be necessary in order to bring about successful development of a culture of positive achievement rather than a concern for inadequacies alone. McClelland (1961) was of the opinion that different peoples, and the same peoples in different periods in their history, have different levels of 'need to achieve'. It would appear that the emphasis is currently on highlighting deficiencies rather than encouraging the full involvement of teachers and lecturers in the quality business. We would argue that quality is an essential part of the process of education, and therefore is largely defined by those involved in the process. There is a wider context in which the process sits, and rather than control from outside we believe that encouragement and rigorous professional dialogue engage teachers in the quality business.

The Changing Context

At present the question of central control still holds back the more wary from shifting resources from concentration upon quality audit. Though there has been a significant shift in the control of education, this has not been recognized in the approach to quality. Perhaps the most important feature at institutional level of the 1986 Education Act lay in the increased power and control exercised by School and College Governing Bodies. Their size and composition was more precisely set down than ever before, so that it became possible to argue in favour of small or large Governing Bodies, and whether the headteacher could better serve the school as a full member or remain as headteacher reporting to the governors. The 1988 Education Reform Act reinforced this distinction and, for instance, gave colleges a choice of between ten and twenty-five members for a 200 full-time-equivalent college, thus raising the debate over the most effective size of Governing Body. To what extent would the College Governing Body be dominated by the up to 50 per cent membership from employment interests, while the LEA was limited to a 30 per cent maximum?

Another highly significant area in which control has changed has come with local financial delegation to individual schools, college and polytechnics. The hiring and firing of staff is now under the jurisdiction of the Governing Body, while the functions of the Local Education Authority have become largely those of oversight and monitoring. For example, in further education, the Training Agency took control of over 25 per cent of funding, with traditional further education provided via the old Rate Support Grant being based on need as determined by central government rather than previous spending levels. The Non Advanced Further Education three-year plans and annual programme revisions have seen their equivalents at the school level in the School Development Plans. The final effects of these changes will only become apparent when the ultimate changes to outside competitive tendering and privatization become commonplace.

The possibility of corporate status for schools as well as colleges has further implications for staff. No extra protection against variations in the education market, and variable pay scales, are only two of a number of areas for possible alteration. Control of land and premises occupied by a school has already become a devolution issue. Undoubtedly central government is reluctant to release its grip upon education – it is a major client, after all. However, our argument is that the time has come to move towards consumer-driven quality with a light-touch quality assurance. Such a move would be in harmony with the devolution that has already taken place.

Analysing these changes and pointing up who has the responsibility for making decisions which affect quality in schools is made easier through a systems model which will identify which core issues can be decided by the different levels controlling the school.

A model originally devised by Andrew Halpin (1957) identifies three distinct arenas of influence and control in those aspects of formulation, adoption, implementation and monitoring/evaluation and review of policies affecting the quality of education. These are the public interest arena, the arena of management or inspection and the process or activity arena.

The public interest arena is usually overseen by government agencies such as central and local government organizations but also includes local members from the governing body of institutions. The management arena is usually occupied by one form of senior management team or another. The third arena is the major activity of the formal organization involved. For us, this is the teaching function in all its forms.

Each component (or column in a diagrammatic representation) of interactions among its three arenas portrays outcomes. These are communicated both upwards and downwards in the columns, and are usually the net result of a series of ritual deliberations in the forms of democracy accepted in the countries being considered in this text.

A number of distinct levels of decision making and control can be identified through the model. In each of these levels, the components or columns are organized so as to relate to one another through a logical, rational and legalized set of procedures. In the European Union context, for example, the public interest groups are:

European Union: the Council of Ministers of the Union

Member State: the UK Parliament and the Department for Education and Employment

Local Authority: the County or Borough Council

School/college: the Governing Body.

The Quality Business

The formal organization component or column for each level contains its own blend and balance of three arenas. In the following example there are four levels, from the European Union itself to the school or college unit, as shown in Table 1.3.

Each arena within a column liaises/interacts/communicates both with its adjacent linked arena at other levels, and also up and down its own column, and additionally with its own external environment.

There exist external agencies to link the different arenas across each of the levels with regular travel across levels within an arena band. For example, officers and inspectors at the LEA level are usually recruited from the ranks of Senior Management Teams in schools and colleges. Some 'variations' bind the linked arenas through cognate moves, for example ministers in Member States move on to work at the European Union in Brussels as commissioners. Membership of external agencies can foster movement between arenas in a single column, or alternatively this is proscribed by custom and practice or by actual legislation.

The process of decision making involves the exchange of scarce resources for unique competencies between generalists and specialists. The roles of inspection and advice 'conflict' at important interfaces between levels and arenas. The question of who should, and who does, control education in a democracy is of importance to all who make some input into or receive the products of the education service. Classifying them into categories of producers and consumers, customers, clients, or those merely engaged in the process of educating, those who have some influence or power and those who have to abide by the decisions of others is the way in which to tease out quality in the field of education – always remembering that defining quality can be a powerful control mechanism in itself.

Table 1.3 Formal organizations in education

Level	European Union	England and Wales	Local Authority	Unit
Educational organization	None to date	DfEE	LEA	School
Arena				
Public interest group	Council of Ministers	Ministers of State	Council committees	Governing body
Management group	European Commissioners	Civil Service OFSTED Inspectors	LEA officers and inspectors	School Senior Management Team
Activity group	Administrative staff	Administrative staff	Advisers, teachers and administrative staff	Teachers and lecturers

Changes will continue to affect the future of educational institutions and the search for quality. Money awaits successful institutions which can manage quality assessments in a consumer-driven manner. Such institutions will attract students like bees round a honey pot.

A Complex Process

The process of managing improvement can be repeated at different levels, but it is important to plan agreement on the reasons, policies and processes for any change as the first stage of reforming a school that is stuck. One that already has identified the need for a drive to enhance quality will already have determined its aim to improve the quality of teaching across the school. It may also have already identified as a goal the way to get as high a rating as possible in any quality assessment exercise. If so, then the starting point may be an objective of introducing policies to ensure these outcomes, and then applying them to guarantee success.

The stages of embedding quality in the process begin with new teachers being given guidance in their early years by experienced teachers appointed as mentors by the headteacher or head of department. Their teaching performance should be subject to regular discussion and review, and any difficulties should be identified and addressed. The head of department should be required to report on teaching ability when a teacher's appointment comes up for renewal or confirmation. A school teaching standards policy should be produced by the school to this end.

After the initial period the teaching performance of members of staff should be reviewed at least every three years, and departments should establish an appropriate procedure for these reviews. The activities reviewed should include class teaching/lecturing, classes and seminars, production of teaching materials, course organization, innovation in content or in teaching methods and work as a tutor or advisor. The results should be discussed with the teacher or lecturer concerned and made available to the head of department, who will be free to make use of such evidence together with student feedback.

For any one individual the scope of information of benefit to an assessment of teaching will start with an audit. This will probably need to include statements relating to the amount and type of teaching undertaken, some comment on the overall planning of that teaching, as well as some observations on classroom effectiveness, innovative teaching or any noteworthy special activities and teaching outcomes.

Objective evidence can be collected regarding the first four of these; the last one is more open to individual judgment. Essentially we are seeking quality in a complex process, and an overanalysis of the process can be stultifying. With this warning in mind it is worth suggesting ways in which teaching can be opened up for positive professional discussion.

Amount and type of teaching undertaken

Each department should be able to state the actual contribution of individual staff members to its organized teaching. Contact hours, type or grade of teaching involved and the individual's workload compared to the general pattern in the department are all factors to be considered.

Classes taught or lectures delivered, marking load, tutorials, practicals, field trips, project supervision, classes seminars, together with any individual supervision of registered research students in the case of university situations can all be assessed.

The amount of teaching by an individual must be considered in relation to other commitments, including administrative jobs.

Most departments have a system of allowances to enable workloads to be compared between staff with different patterns of activity. The information required for a teaching profile needs to be given over several years, and not only for the current year.

Overall planning of teaching

Activity other than direct classroom teaching needs to be considered. Valuable examples will include items such as:

- planning the delivery of the syllabus (usually a group activity)
- revision and updating of course material
- effective arrangements for practical and written work
- efficiency in setting and marking tests and exams
- provision of good tutorial support and accessibility to students

The evidence of a person's standard of achievement in these areas will come from information at departmental or school level – some of which will be confidential in nature – which may often be supported by peer review and observation of teaching.

Classroom effectiveness and personal teaching ability – in lectures, seminars, tutorials, practical classes in the case of higher education – will be shown through well-prepared and structured sessions, with presentation of material achieved clearly and audibly, with the use of teaching aids where appropriate and with an ability to promote and guide class discussions.

Evidence about teaching and lecturing ability comes from direct classroom observation together with student questionnaires taken from older students. It is more difficult to assess small-group teaching, and questionnaires are not entirely satisfactory for small numbers. General discussion with students, and self-assessment, can also elicit information on teaching ability.

For beginning teachers and lecturers, the above headings will cover the main teaching activities. They will be encouraged throughout to take part in a professional dialogue about their role in the process of education.

Innovation and special activities will be of more relevance to established staff. There can be an expectation that contributions to teaching have been made through a number of different ways. The design of new courses or major restructuring of existing ones, innovation in methods of teaching or assessment, together with any substantial academic counselling, also need recording. The development of special courses, the publication of textbook or journal articles on teaching and learning in school and higher education or in a subject discipline, together with any involvement with computer assisted learning or distance learning, will be valuable guidelines to quality enhancement of the school by utilizing readily available expertise if this is made known through the development review system. In other words, these activities should be listed by members of staff on CVs, and the department should also have records of them.

Teaching outcomes

These are a little more difficult to describe. Good teaching at all education levels will have elements of depth and intellectual challenge which cannot be quantified and which will influence students in different ways.

Some of these might centre on a large take-up of any optional courses given, or on the ability to attract research students from a university. The member of staff may be offering effective help to junior teachers, obtaining LEA interest or external funding for teaching projects. The standard measures of the performance of students in assessed work also play an important part, while it may be appropriate to consider the subsequent careers of the teacher's students. The assessment of this area is largely a matter of judgment, based upon peer review and discussion in the forums concerned, with external examiners' reports being appropriate in higher education.

These procedures should provide a picture of ability and performance, indicating areas of strengths and helping to identify any need for development. Development review of the school is best if applied gradually to foster commitment. Overall school agreement is the first target, with departmental agreement following, a start being made with heads of department undergoing peer review.

Team teaching experiences add to the interest each teacher builds into their own teaching styles and performances, starting with individual sessions, or with related parts/sessions of the course. The preparation and review of teaching will focus interest on these matters naturally; team teaching and departmental meetings are further ways of enhancing the professional dialogue.

Mentoring roles have already been mentioned as ways to enhance effectiveness, and it remains important to determine what 'Quality' means to the individual teacher. An exercise in debating issues from the point of view of the school and its community can be useful here. The issue of quality should always be on the agenda of all involved.

Quality in the Future

The educational institution of the future may be served by high-powered educational computer networks managed by an information technology organization. The institution's premises are likely to be built, maintained and owned by an outside company, and leased to the institution when needed – rented to conferences and summer schools separately. Cleaning and caretaking is already outsourced in many institutions today, along with the provision of students' meals. Teachers, headteachers, governors and secretarial services will be more efficiently serviced by centralized units. Home workers will be more in vogue, with teachers submitting work requirements and home workers supplying the work to be taught, while marking is completed by outworkers. Sports facilities, student union premises and activities will all be under the control of their respective bodies, but may well be provided centrally. The days of the individual bespoke school or college are numbered – but quality will determine those that succeed and those fail or are absorbed. The success of any institution in such a world must depend upon its ability to provide consumer-driven quality. In essence the process is more important than the structures by which it is currently delivered.

Ways to succeed include greater emphasis on a versatile policy for staff development which can cope with constant flux, and a communications audit constantly under review – memos and newsletters to all those both inside and outside the school are important here. Techniques of marketing apply to all staff, full time and part time, teaching and support; for example, receptionists with detailed knowledge of how an institution works will be needed so that learners are welcomed and encouraged.

Business sponsorship is likely to become accepted as a norm, including the secondment of teachers and lecturers for work experience, so that those receiving the output from the schools will be able to influence the processes more appropriately – perhaps through business or industrial sponsorships. Above all, the issues of budgeting and spending patterns can no longer be expected to be secret. Instead, managers will need to become increasingly trained in industrial relations, employment law, publicity and marketing.

The change inherent in such a new world is frightening, but demands a flexible response. A centrally controlled, mechanistic system will not respond to change effectively. It is vital that the search for quality in education, as we have defined it, is properly managed (Fullan with Stiegelbanner, 1991). As Machiavelli wrote in *The Prince*:

> A man who neglects what is actually done for what should be done paves the way to self-destruction rather than self-preservation.

2 Inspecting It In is Out

> Evidence...presented by Don Foster, Liberal Democrat Education spokesman to the Commons Education Select Committee, demonstrates that schools inspected during 1993–1997 showed less improvement than those that remained uninspected.
> (Bright, M., *The Observer*, 23 August 1998, p. 16)

> The introduction of the Office for Standards in Education in 1993 was a watershed, not only for teachers but for inspectors too. When OFSTED announced that contracts would be awarded competitively, a multi-million pound industry sprang from nowhere. With the contract to inspect just one school earning as much as £26,000 there was a huge incentive for former civil servants to become thrusting entrepreneurs.
> (*Times Educational Supplement*, 19 December 1997, p. 7)

The issue of quality in education has been high on political agendas recently, and following the intentions of the new Labour government we have addressed the main issues involved in this process as it has affected schools, colleges and universities. For our money, inspecting quality into education is just not possible, whether through OFSTED inspections in schools, Quality Assessments by the Higher Education Funding Council for England (HEFCE) in Higher Education, or just plain Charter Marks such as Investors in People UK. What are the alternatives for the new era? Or, to quote from the title of an article in *Education Today*, 'Who Inspects the Inspectors?' (Lowenstein, 1996).

In reality, we find a lack of conviction on the part of assessors to draw together often disparate threads to produce a coherent model for the enhancement of students' learning experiences. Perhaps that is to be expected, as only the few who see these matters as counter-productive and problematic offer suggestions for improvement in any way. This chapter looks at the quality industry from the perspective of two different models – whole school inspection in the OFSTED mode, and the current HEFC Quality Council subject assessments procedures – to see how both aim for quality enhancement, but fail. The alternative way of building a self-developing quality culture is advocated as the only effective route to successful enhancement of performance in education.

The Language of Inspection

The aim of inspection is to promote value for money in public investment, accountability for public money, and competition between institutions. The processes in schools and those in universities differ, in that the OFSTED inspection assumes a deficiency model through the imposition of the action plan for improvement, with tight deadlines for its implementation by school governors following the end of the inspection. The required school post-inspection action plan sets out ways in which the improvement agenda will be managed and followed through. The HEFC Quality Council, on the other hand, starts with a self-assessment profile written six months before the subject-based assessment commences. University academic departments are then assessed against their own stated aims and objectives. Both activities are based on the same endeavour – the pursuit of evidence. This evidence is all too often taken to be hard as rock, whereas it is, in reality, no more than sand. It is sand because value judgments are an integral part of evidence gathered from the process of teaching and learning. As Maurice Holt (1981) has pointed out, 'Education, then, is "par excellence" a field in which everything depends on value judgements. There is no value-free evaluation, no easy way of judging curriculum activity.'

The present terminology for school inspection, in our view, confuses two dissimilar aspects of this activity. Quality is to do with the process of the students' experience, whereas standards relate to a pre-determined scale with which to measure quality in terms of the output of the learning process. So it is confusing to require inspectors to report on, among other things, the quality of the education provided by the school and the educational standards achieved in the school (DfEE, 1995a, p. 8) as though these both varied from school to school. Both exercises should address the quality of the learning process. Quality should be raised in relation to set fixed standards. The OFSTED *Handbook* says, however, that 'The inspection process should help the school to raise educational standards' (1995a, p. 10). In schools, the focus of the terminology used should be on meeting set standard targets for learning output. In colleges and university subject department assessments, there is more consistency in terminology, although here again a confusion with grades for different aspects of the quality of the process are couched in output scales. Page 43 of the 'Handbook' is still confused over what quality is, though it makes the aim of the inspection exercise a little clearer when it says:

> Provision, or the quality of education provided, is covered in five sections, and should be evaluated in terms of its contribution to the

outcomes. Teaching is the major factor contributing to pupils' attainment, progress and response. Thorough evaluation of its quality and its impact on the educational standards achieved by pupils is, therefore, central to inspection.

(OFSTED, 1995, p. 43)

For consistency, any report should evaluate the quality of a school's learning processes against set standards, by assessing the achievements of the pupils. At least in the nineteenth-century 'Payment by Results' system of inspection, reports were consistent in their use of 'standards' to signify the set targets against which the achievements of each class group were measured.

In response to demands for greater public accountability for the national investment in education, schools strive to demonstrate higher achievement against the standards of success. Nevertheless, there are those who would make unfavourable comparisons between the quality of education in this country and that of other competitor nations. If we are to continue to compete successfully in a global economy, we need to demonstrate that the quality of our own educational provision can rival our international competitors.

Inspection has been hailed as the means to improvements without serious consideration being given to the exact nature of regular independent inspection by OFSTED. The subtitle of OFSTED's 1993 Corporate Plan reads 'Improvement through Inspection'. Surely such a statement must be challenged and greater definition of the activity demanded. In Lewis Carroll's *Through the Looking Glass*, Humpty Dumpty explained the meaning of the word 'slithy' to Alice, saying: 'You see it's like a portmanteau – there are two meanings picked up into one word.' Inspection is such a portmanteau word, and its exact meaning depends upon where the inspectors stand on the continuum from quality assurance to quality development. Where they stand will influence the role or roles they play. The role has been described by Bolam (1982) as a Janus role. However, Wilcox and Gray (1996) have teased out four roles: those of evaluator, controller, auditor and interactive communicator. The use of the term 'inspector' as a procedure to impose quality while neither defining carefully what is meant, nor taking into account the complexity of the teaching and learning process, is merely reciting a mantra.

Furthermore, what do different people mean by the term 'quality' when it is applied to education (see Chapter 1)? Is it not better considered as 'a way by which children gain in self-esteem rather than lose it' (Lowenstein, 1996) than compared with consumer goods, where the market is attracted by the best quality at the keenest prices? Goods of high quality may carry connotations of affluence, prosperity and opulence; when we think of quality generally, we associate it with expense – we think of 'the best' regardless of cost. Yet quality is by no means synonymous with expense or luxury. Otherwise 'cheap quality' would be a contradiction in terms (P.A. Consulting Group, 1992). Quality in today's consumer-oriented society has become associated with fulfilling client expectations, and 'quality', 'value' and 'choice' are a central part of the consumer dogma in relation to goods and services. Quality has thus become the watchword of the consumer creed, and is enshrined in consumer charters. However, we need to be on guard, since the use of words is a subtle and complicated exercise as meanings change (Mullen, 1977). At present, there is confusion when the term is applied to education. Was it ever thus?

The answer to that question is probably 'yes'. Comment showed that considerations of quality in education were being compromised over fifty years ago because, as Thompson and Reeves (1947) wrote, the concept was bedevilled by the 'habit of quantitative thinking which has entered educational discussion and now pervades it'.

By 1998, quantitative measures had become a benchmark of quality in educational provision: for example in the comparative tables of ranked test and examination results in UK schools. It is a commonplace maxim with the attendant overuse, and hence trivialization, of the term 'quality'. However, it is clearly something which – to most people's minds – schools, colleges and universities ought to be able to demonstrate. It is now defined in the sense of responding to the needs of the consumer: applying market principles deemed to be a force to stimulate the development of quality. The Conservative government made clear its belief in 1992 (Department for Education, 1992b) that quality is increased through greater accountability, and that parental rights need to be enhanced; or, as paragraph 1.66 put it: 'In many cases parental wishes through choice of school will drive improvements.'

The public perception of quality is a determining influence when finance is tied to choices made by consumers. This perception needs careful examination when market strategies are being devised. Quality is here being defined with reference to the user of the service. This is 'reactive' quality: responding under pressure to external demands in a climate of decreasing confidence in the work of schools, colleges and universities. Media headlines proclaiming the 'incompetence' of some teachers and headteachers create news, yet they seriously damage the image of the profession. More important, they detract from the quality mission that many institutions now pursue.

In the second phase of OFSTED inspections, schools previously inspected in the first round will be assessed on the improvements achieved in the development of quality since the first inspection. Here quality must be concerned with managing the process of change to effect the advancements necessary to bring about improvement. This requires proactive approaches to quality management and a strategic capability. A strategic approach to developing quality is the best safeguard, and acts as an anchor to hold the institution firm in its own core purposes, rather than being directionless, pushed and pulled in response to the competing pressures of current ideology or societal demands. Strategic planning allows the institution to chart the ocean in a way which accords with its own emergent vision, rather than being blinded by a vision from above. When the institution itself is clear about what it hopes to accomplish, the likelihood of being manoeuvred and controlled by turbulence in the environment, or drifting, helpless, at the latest whim of those who seek to exert influence and pressure, is significantly diminished.

If quality development is to become proactive, a certain dynamism is required on the part of the institution. This should anticipate likely future events and demands, and consider the implications for institutional strategy. Such an approach sees strategy not as something firm and fixed, but as a versatile instrument which can be employed to the institution's own advantage, enabling it to exercise manoeuvrability in the face of impending changes. Strategic leadership today needs to anticipate unstable and unsettling environments while maintaining its task of purposefully moving towards greater effectiveness. Deming has made clear in the third of his fourteen points (1982) that the need for mass inspection must be eliminated by building quality into any product in the first place.

Improvement is a learning process involving refining, revisiting and rethinking existing practices. At best it will have continued professional development at its foundation. Training in new skills and new ways of thinking are required. This is part of the evolutionary process of learning and changing. A capacity to reflect is essential if quality is to be improved. It demands a painful process of self-examination involving honesty, openness and an acknowledgement that professional colleagues can learn from one another. Initiatives such as Guidelines for the Review and Internal Development of Schools (GRIDS) can be seen as a move towards the development of a learning culture through rigorous self-review and self-examination informing future development. Hopkins (1987) is categorical on this point:

> School evaluation, for example, when practised within the GRIDS framework becomes a powerful tool for school improvement. However, when school evaluation is conceptualized within an accountability framework it produces little evidence of school improvement and indeed tends to inhibit it.

He goes on to say that the ability to learn how to change is probably more important than the change itself – reminiscent of the old saying that it is better to teach people how to fish than merely provide them with fish to eat. This creates the internal capability to put the institution in charge of change, to chart a course for itself towards improvement (Hoy and Wood, 1993).

Inspecting It In is Out

In learning organizations, people are continually expanding their capabilities to shape their future, with change or improvement demanding that individuals learn how to do something new. The development of quality can now be seen directly in relation to the internal capacity to learn.

The OFSTED school inspection arrangements were founded on an accountability framework. That was clear right from the start, as the instructing letter from the (then) education secretary to the (then) chief inspector of schools stated:

> You will be playing a key part in the reforms foreshadowed by the Parent's Charter which open up the education service to detailed and regular public scrutiny....The hard and public evidence from the inspections you are to arrange will provide all schools with an incentive for improvement, as well as setting their agenda for action.
> (Department for Education, 1992a)

That rationale proceeded from a belief that inspection can lead to improvement:

> The purpose of inspection is to identify strengths and weaknesses so that schools may improve the quality of education they provide and raise the educational standards achieved by their pupils. The published report and summary report provide information for parents and the local community about the quality and standards of the school, consistent with the requirements of the Parents' Charter. The inspection process, feedback and reports give direction to the school's strategy for planning, review and improvement by providing rigorous external evaluation and identifying key issues for action.
> (DfEE, 1995a, p. 8)

School inspection in providing a public account of the work of the schools would, it was envisaged, lend direction to improvement through the provision of an agenda for action. What was never realized – never mind bridged – was the gap between being 'provided with' an agenda for action, and the concept of development of quality in any learning organization. We believe that quality in education is 'constructed out of a painstaking dialogue, rather than imposed from above' (Institute for Public Policy Relations, 1993). It would seem that others now believe that too:

> You don't increase education standards by declaration
> (Kenneth Baker, former Minister of Education, commenting on BBC1 TV, 2 May 1997, 9:30 am)

By appointing a Minister for Standards in Education, the new Labour

Inspecting It In is Out

government appeared in one respect to be perpetuating its predecessor's errors by confusing standards (which are set by government) with quality (which is achieved by the institutions themselves). Accountability is informed by both parties agreeing procedures for monitoring quality in relation to the standards set. It is to be hoped that the Fryer Report recommendations on Lifelong Learning will result in the promotion of teacher involvement in quality enhancement on a common front, from schools through colleges to universities (Department for Education and Employment, 1997b). One suspects that the National Council for the Inspection of Schools suggested by Ted Wragg and Tim Brighouse in 1995 will prove to be an equally useful animal. After all, as Deming (1982) stated in the eighth of his fourteen points, it is vital that an organization should 'drive out fear'. Effective two-way communication helps everybody to work more effectively and more productively.

Motivation is an important factor here, and one to which insufficient attention has been directed. The successful management of change involves gaining commitment, which is borne from a belief in the value of the proposed change. A culture of 'naming and shaming' is not helpful in promoting the pursuit of excellence. Professional development is enhanced more effectively through the recognition of effort. Such endeavour is an important factor in developing quality, as Allen (1995) noted when he wrote: 'The important thing is that it is done on their own, not imposed from outside. No one likes to have someone continually pointing out their weaknesses.'

> Guide them, help them, but don't sit on them or smother them. 'I sat on piglet once' said Pooh, 'By accident. He didn't much care for it'. 'Few do' said Owl.
>
> (Allen, 1995)

A key aspect of the process is trust: trust that skilled and effective professional colleagues will strive for excellence in their practice without the pressure of public accountability. Whether this is the false consciousness inherent in Marxist ideology or the Holy Grail of the Christian venture is discussed in the final chapter.

There is an essential message – to centre improvement within the institution, encouraging the institution to develop its own momentum for improvement by allowing teachers the professional space to do the job. The case study schools in Chapter 6 present examples of school-generated momentum for improvement. The LEAs in these cases acted as critical friends, having confidence in the schools to improve through their own endeavour. Improvement is school centred with the critical friend asking tough questions, prompting reflection on practice, questioning and probing assumptions, recognising effort, disseminating good practice and enhancing professional skill and expertise. The critical friend does not prescribe but recognizes that improvement comes from evolutionary development rather than being something which follows from addressing the outcomes of an external audit.

The previous pattern, in place since 1992, for further and higher education was changed in 1998. However, there is little hope that its successor will differ much from the burdensome, tiring, intrusive, invalid inspection assessment. A wise combination of audit and assessment practices may be achieved in higher education, although the expectation is that the new body will add the Quality Audit procedures to the Higher Education Funding Council's model. What is needed is a focus on advice, on ways to offer suggestions and support for those improvements in place of the regime of inspection, rather than the overbearing authority of the inspectors with their emphasis on so-called standards; instead, there should be a sense of identification with the nature of the learning process. More empathy, and certainly more informality in the assessment procedures, would, in our view, produce a self-developing climate. Further changes planned may be more developmental in nature.

How can Quality Work for Education?

Do Charter Marks, discussed in Chapter 1, offer any salvation? While the terminology of competitive advantage and competitive edge is scattered about the Investors in People (IiP) literature, there is a surprising dearth of references to quality other than to the business enterprises established to oversee Quality with a capital Q. These include the National Vocational Qualifications, National Targets for Education and Training, the Management Charter Initiative, Total Quality Management and the National Training Awards. As with BS 5750, IiP is primarily business and industry oriented, where customers want to know that the produce they are buying will not harm them in use. This is of little importance to schools and universities, where, in our opinion, improvements in internal quality can come more readily from enhancing the possibilities of the self-developing climate. After all, when the inspectors and assessors depart, it is the people who are left who have to devise strategies, implement ideas and put into practice their own ideologies of success if their institution is to prosper in this competitive age.

The quality industry has developed in a series of stages: first we had quality control concerned with detection, then came quality assurance aimed at prevention, followed by total quality management systems – focused on continuous quality improvement. What is now needed, and was expected from the new Labour-appointed ministerial team at the DfEE, is the development of new strategies aimed at problem solving and opportunity finding. So far the only opportunity finding has been personal, with the rapid rise of Stephen Byers from School Standards Minister to Chief

Inspecting It In is Out

Secretary at the Treasury, and then on to Secretary of State for Trade and Industry. However, Figure 2.1 shows how the general pattern of quality development can be represented.

The diagram shows the development of new quality standards as the outcome of a substantial process of evaluation in the quality business. These independently stated abstract standards alone can guarantee the enhancement of Total Quality Management systems, where the common outcomes from real situations can be accommodated within an overall framework. The emergence of quality assurance rather than quality control of these outcomes was a great stride forward. Previously there existed only the concept of a final 'putting right' in the end those things that were known to be in error part-way through the stages of the process. With quality assurance there was no need to wait until the final outcome, and with it rejection for some or all of the batch because of imperfections. The programming of corrections during the process became possible instead. Everything was vouched for throughout the process, as it moved from one stage to the next. Needless to say, inspection after the event cannot 'inspect' quality into the process. This was where Total Quality Management systems were needed, to oversee each of the separate activities as the process unfolded. Although, as

Figure 2.1   Quality development and quality concerns

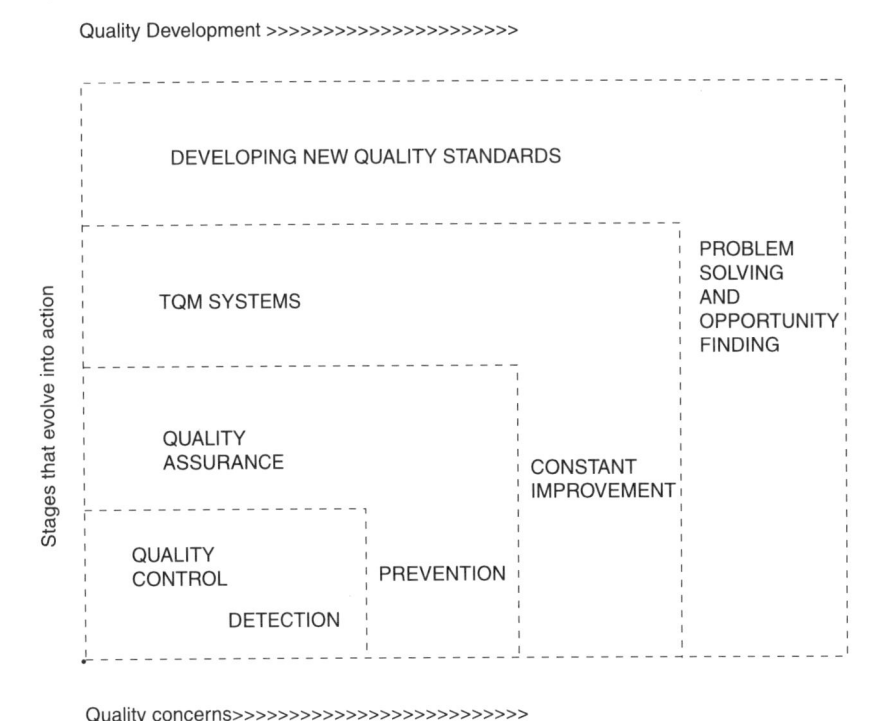

Quality Development >>>>>>>>>>>>>>>>>>>>>>>

```
                    DEVELOPING NEW QUALITY STANDARDS

                                                           PROBLEM
                                                           SOLVING
                    TQM SYSTEMS                            AND
                                                           OPPORTUNITY
                                                           FINDING

   Stages that
   evolve into      QUALITY
   action           ASSURANCE                  CONSTANT
                                               IMPROVEMENT

                    QUALITY
                    CONTROL         PREVENTION
                         DETECTION
```

Quality concerns>>>>>>>>>>>>>>>>>>>>>>>>>>>>

35

Inspecting It In is Out

Maurice Holt has pointed out in the Introduction to this book, Deming disliked the term 'total quality management'. He considered the process to be organic and complex, rather than procedural and linear. 'Total quality management' was certainly not a sufficient answer.

At the same time there was an increase in concern about Quality itself. At first this process was seen as one of detecting errors which were there in the system. This moved on to addressing these errors through prevention, and later introduced the concept of continuous improvement. Finally there is the chance to create the science of problem solving and even to move towards opportunity finding as the vehicles with which to confront quality issues even before they have begun to be addressed in the present context. What is offered here is the possibility of targeting developments to meet the needs of the future concerns over quality.

This is certainly not the stage currently reached by inspection of schools and colleges. That may be their overall aim for the future, but right now the targets are to confront problems by naming poor performers, in the expectation that somehow they will improve their performance, with some degree of tuning, for a future inspection to confirm. The relationship between what needs to be addressed by which elements in the educational partnership is represented in Figure 2.2, a three-way diagram expressing a balanced concern for educational development.

Figure 2.2 Balanced concern for educational development

Government Funding

◄--►
Education   The
Community   Market

This relationship has now changed dramatically. While the premise is still accepted that:

> A nation's competitive advantage depends on the skills and inventiveness of its people. The importance of this to business success is universally recognized,

the conclusions are not so obvious, since:

> ...there remains a gap between recognition and taking action to provide a working environment which encourages the continuous development of people.

Neither is the prescription:

> Through improved performance, Investor in People organisations develop a competitive edge to secure their future prosperity and create an improved skill base which allows business objectives to be expanded
> (Investors in People UK, 1996)

It is interesting to note that there is not a word about quality, or about inspecting quality into the business, as enshrined in OFSTED literature.

The four IiP principles of commitment, planning, action and evaluating use terminology which is both tautological and confused. In particular, three of the four principles define themselves in terms of goals – the generic term for defined intended outcomes – while the fourth, action, talks of programme. In detail these four principles are elaborated as:

- COMMITMENT to investing in people to achieve business goals
- PLANNING how skills of individuals and teams are to be developed to achieve these goals
- ACTION to develop and use necessary skills in a well-defined and continuing programme; and
- EVALUATION of progress towards goals, value achieved and future needs

Further confusion abounds when IiP describes itself as both a standard and a framework for continuous improvement. The five steps which will help an organization to move from its existing position to achieving the IiP Standard are described as:

1. Review
2. Action
3. Assessment
4. Achievement
5. Continuous improvement

The Assessment is carried out by an external 'qualified independent assessor' from the local Assessment Unit. This assessment has two parts: a review of the completeness and relevance of the documentary evidence, and an on-site visit.

The IiP Planning Principle 2 demands clear goals and targets for the organization. There is a recognition that different terminology exists in different organizations, such as aims and objectives, but IiP then seek to clarify the wording by contrasting goals 'which may be aspirational' with 'targets [that] should at least be specific, measurable and time bound'.

Targets do not appear separately in the lengthy glossary of terms used, though objectives do and are used in the definition of 'Goals and targets' which are identified as a linked concept.

To add even more to the confusion of terminology in the explanation of 'Goals and targets', the literature states that:

> 'Objectives' is used in place of 'goals and targets' to clarify the point that the specific outcomes sought from training and development may not necessarily be the same as planned levels of performance for the organisation, teams and individuals.

'Objectives' themselves are defined as:

> the outcomes which are sought from a specified action or set of actions. Good objectives are specific, measurable, agreed, realistic and time bound. Training and development objectives can relate to the desired level of performance required as a result of training and development actions.

The important omission here is that no timescale order is associated with the process. We prefer the well-proven pattern of Policy Formulation, Adoption, Implementation, and Review as identified by us in an earlier publication (Hoy and Wood, 1993) using the model of aims, goals and objectives. This has the advantage of identifying and giving values to the different stages in the implementation of a plan, and the various levels at which decisions regarding implementation of plans take place. For example, a plan to enhance and encourage quality in education may be taken by a 'commitment', as Investors in People term it, at the most senior level, but entirely fail to be implemented through, to and by the junior ranks.

We also prefer to identify a series of time-related outcomes – in IiP terminology 'goals and targets' – which are planned to be achieved in stages, over a period of time that may be no more than loosely set out. It is this time-related staging which in our view acts as the catalyst for the process of delivery of the achievement itself, and with it the assurance that the 'goals and targets' will be reached. We define the process as follows, where the word 'target' is used as the generic term for all intended outcomes:

Policy Aims: longer-term targets of a strategic nature.

Personal and Professional Goals: recognizable medium-term specific stages on the way towards the aims. They are identified as tactical plans.

Objectives: short-term targets used to make more specific the operational purposes of the plan.

If we are to follow Deming's precepts and not only improve processes but also constantly improve the design of a product or service, then we should consider carefully his approach to built-in quality. There can be no 'instant pudding', and it will take time for quality to be built into the educational process at institutional level. Yet the lesson is clear from the literature on quality in manufacturing and commerce: you cannot inspect quality in, you can only encourage all those involved in any enterprise to build quality into the processes from the beginning.

3 Quality Enhancement Through Development Review

The greatest difference between the philosophy inherent in the new inspection system and that of its predecessors lies in the way schools are being required to conform to standard procedures, instead of being allowed to pursue their own interpretation of quality and value. In this complex and rapidly changing world, based upon efficiency and value for money, institutions now more than ever before need to maintain their competitive edge through pursuing their own interpretation of quality and value standards.

Schools 'shamed' as failing schools do not suddenly outperform their previous best. Far from it; instead they go through a traumatic and disruptive period of anxiety lasting several years. Then, in all probability, the schools climb back to near their existing levels, and continue to show the modest improvements of which they were capable in the first place, before the 'naming and shaming' identity hit them and knocked them off target. *The Observer* of 23 August 1998 published an assessment of the statistics of success as measured by the DfEE GCSE Grades achieved by the first few schools in this unenviable category. This assessment underlines the lack of improvement made.

The crucial question is, can we count on the support of those who deliver the service, be they teachers in the classroom or lecturers in the laboratories, to develop their competencies when the inspectors are long gone? Conformity to common standards will only ensure a benchmark threshold level of provision – the essential feature of government in such arenas as health and safety, common decency and legal entitlements. Schools, colleges and universities are much more in the business of enhancement than mere compliance implies. Some people may think it pertinent to the mediocre, the mundane and the monotonous, to set exacting standards for all; but this is no response to the needs of individual institutions who wish to surpass those set criteria – or even to diverge from them to offer a detour of delight in some more rewarding areas of life.

New developments in teaching and the assessment of that teaching must be in harmony with the evaluation made by consumers and clients. The insistence on conformity to standard procedures so as to meet the demands of clients in terms of measurable output unbalances the procedure, so that the consumers have no involvement in the process. Students remember the moments when their thinking was developed and enhanced by skilled teaching. They do not remember the school's performance under inspection or its particular place on national league tables.

It is not only OFSTED that has taken up the stance of demanding conformity. The adoption of the new six-part strategy set out by the Quality Assurance Agency looks towards ever tighter tolerance levels, beloved of engineers of old. In future the Quality Assurance Agency will in all probability require Qualifications in Higher Education to adhere to 'templates' setting out clearer descriptions of the content and aims of their courses, with 'benchmark' standards more clearly defined in terms of the abilities and attributes expected of graduates – differing from subject to subject for instance, and with threshold standards seen as the minimum. These will be checked by registered external examiners to compare standards across a list of 41 subject areas.

Institutional Codes of Practice on such matters as quality assurance, public information and standards, student support and guidance, overseas students, collaborative work and post-graduate work will be required of Higher Education providers. The codes, of course, will need to be universally valid and applicable. The Quality Assurance Agency intends to do this by focusing on results, rather than on how these results are achieved. Yet the process of learning is the essence of any educational institution, and, as in life itself, there is no standard pattern of schooling.

Clearly, this lacks a process for sustainable improvement; rather it is based upon the assumption that quality is in some way co-terminous with compliance to standard procedures and numerical mechanisms. Deviation from such routines is to be punished by reduction of income or withdrawal of accreditation – a negative reward system if ever there was one!

Quality for the present, and the previous, government seems concerned more with compliance than with anything else. It lacks identification with improvement, and appears to be based on the military 'kit inspection' model. As long as everything is laid out neatly and in order, all is well with the school, and woe betide the institution without the approved shine on its image, the regulatory data on its 'successes' for the inspectors to note in their reports. Commercial discipline – if that is what is being sought by government – does not come this way.

A system of market forces would provide parents and students with a wide array of provision from which to choose, with the implication that those lacking in quality and not able to provide their clients with what they desire would wither away. But this has supply implications and is something governments are reluctant to provide out of the public purse. Perhaps in the end governments want power, and they want to be able to manage education to enhance their own reputations, not to provide their publics with a better service. One way to achieve both ends is through valuing development of staff in schools. This is not catered for by set-piece inspections and reports – which in the quest for conformity in aims and learning outcomes have an adverse effect on the ability and flair of individual teachers. Some recognition of the need to support action plans has been made, however, by changing the balance of supply and training grants.

Improving efficiency and eliminating waste in education is not part of the vocabulary of quality as currently practised. If the vast quantity of documentation demanded of the quality process is anything to go by, the exercise is more about conformity than development. Cost consciousness and an emphasis on the importance of its staff to any enterprise are qualities behind the great names in the High Street – rather than of the government education service. Initiatives, specialist services, particular sector developments are the name of the game of continual improvement, and these are a world away from meticulously conforming to standards set by outsiders to the business.

In the current economic climate, the quality of a school's output, the performance of its teachers and the efficiency of its management are all the more important. Some have gone down the performance route, while others, including ourselves, believe in the need for an alternative to performance management. In Deming's (1982) words: 'Quality comes not from inspection but from improvement of the production process.'

Performance management as a process to evaluate and improve individual and whole-school performance in order to achieve agreed objectives is laudable in theory, but experience has shown that in practice most schools are not getting the best out of this approach. Often a lack of commitment and understanding on the part of teachers themselves, together with poor coordination and implementation from the senior staff, leads to failure.

It is essential that there is total commitment to the process of review and development. The understanding by teachers of what has to be done to improve the chances of successful learning within the school has to be developed. It has to be made clear that the purpose of the exercise is to increase their professional satisfaction from doing their job effectively as part of a dynamic organization. A clear picture must be painted identifying the problems and recognizing the skills needed to tackle these. Training must be provided so that the problems can be overcome. When teachers are involved in the identification of the problems that act as a barrier to quality learning, and are then supported in gaining the skills needed to deal with these blocks, they will respond positively to management.

Quality enhancement if it is to become sustainable needs some process behind it that conforms to staff expectations and allows them to identify with its purpose, so that it becomes their own and not some imposed prescriptive demand. The need is to enhance the provision of the education service, not merely to safeguard it from the incompetent few. Of course it is true that these few may well be weeded out by the universal process of setting a standard approach to the commonsense values of the service. However, applying this approach repeatedly across the whole service will not set growth in motion.

The processes of supervision, mentoring and the adoption of a critical friend in the development review processes can and do enhance quality – but in very different ways and with differing success rates. However, unlike the inspection industry, these processes are not seen as a thorn in the side of the established order of things. On the contrary, they are welcomed by those professionals who have an agenda for action that encompasses the enhancement of quality in their own work. They ensure thought-provoking discussions and activities separated from any report writing, from any harsh judgment and hence from stressful encounters with 'experts' in the procedures of examining success and commenting on its absence in a certain field.

Adopting as the terminology for supervision the vocabulary of social work, supervision is the process – generally exercised by an older and more experienced person – by which to guide a younger and less experienced person through a process. It is a responsibility which consists of the act of enquiring and assessing another's performance with a view to assisting that person to examine their own practice. It is a formative assessment, as distinct from the summative assessment of some teaching output. It may be undertaken through observation, but is more readily applied away from the scene, often in a private conversation originated by the one whose practice is to be considered. It is formative because it is diagnostic in nature, whereas a summative assessment will produce a definitive statement, a final testimonial to the work the individual has been charged with doing. There is the sense of continuing to improve, of striving to achieve, from a formative assessment which is essentially provisional and dependent upon the immediate and longer-term steps to be taken by the practitioner to enhance their own work in their own ways. There is no requirement to conform, to practise in precisely the ways favoured by the supervisor. This allows the competent practitioner to explore other modes and methods of obtaining what for them are worthwhile targets in their professional development. At the same time the supervisor is not a goad, or someone incessantly at loggerheads with current practice, because they recognize sincerely that there are different ways to enhance effectiveness, and that no one method has the prerequisite accolade of guaranteed success in all cases (Bennett and Galton, 1976).

Supervision takes time. It is slow, it is thought-provoking, its impact is, however, longlasting and depends for its success on the workability of pairs, or even teams, of competent and confident practitioners in the same field. It requires the time and opportunity for them to sit down together to provide this essential feedback and discussion of their philosophies and practices.

By contrast, coaching is a one-to-one real-time activity. It is good for improving the ability of the employee to perform a specific task. Its acceptability lies in the mutual recognition and understanding that one party has the expertise to recommend precise actions to be taken which will enhance the effectiveness of the other in their current practice in the classroom or lecture theatre. There is a place for such coaching, no doubt, but it is predicated on the availability of an expert teacher with the perceptive knowledge of how to apply the remedy to a staff member in a particular practice.

Mentoring is more popular at present, as it provides a link and continual personal development contact between training and development and the personal initiatives of an individual teacher/lecturer. The term 'evaluation' is reserved as a final statement of the outcomes of some enquiry into the effectiveness of a course or programme of study delivered to a learner. It is not related to how well the leaner has performed, but rather to the degree of success registered by the programme in terms of its stated aims, goals and objectives. It relates essentially to the degree to which the learning outcomes were satisfactorily pre-defined. It naturally has its limitations, as there are outcomes that are not predictable and there are those which are unpredictable over time.

The essential difference between the three processes of supervision, coaching and mentoring, as compared to that of inspection, lies in the extent to which the procedures are adopted voluntarily by staff. The process may be required by management, but its execution is left to the best intents of the practitioners themselves, much as in the counselling realm. A check is made of both parties to ensure that the process is being undertaken, and no more. Certainly no reports of encounters are required to ensure its effectiveness. That comes from a recognition by the practitioners themselves of the worth and value of the processes, of their effectiveness in meeting the real needs of the client group, and an understanding that the process is rooted in the professional requirements of teachers and lecturers as part of their commitment to value for money for their clients. It is this aspect that gives a sustainability dimension. There is a personal outcome, a professional increment. At the same time the school benefits too, since each worker has a stake in the outcome of the whole service. Where the individual sees benefits to themselves, the institution also gains not just incrementally but exponentially, as each additional benefit accrues through the work of every other member of the team in that service.

The Role of the Mentor

This is perhaps best described in diagrammatic form as a continuum between one or other in control of the development of the mentee. This is shown in Figure 3.1.

Mentoring in its various forms is a formal way of supporting colleagues to develop their work over a period of time. In an age of rapid change and

Figure 3.1   Mentoring roles

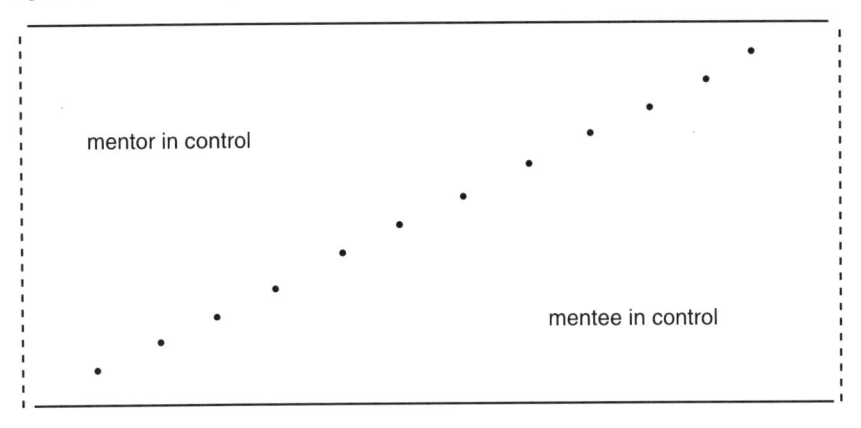

```
┌─────────────────────────────────────────────────┐
│                                          •      │
│                                       •         │
│  mentor in control                 •            │
│                                 •               │
│                             •                   │
│                         •                       │
│                     •                           │
│                 •         mentee in control     │
│           •                                     │
│       •                                         │
│   •                                             │
└─────────────────────────────────────────────────┘
```

The role of the mentor is to:

- question, to elicit facts;
- give advice on career development;
- confront and discuss current issues;
- take the lead and make decisions at least early on in the relationship.

and to encourage the mentee to;

- clarify understanding;
- challenge own assumptions;
- consider different perspectives;
- make decisions for maximizing the outcome of the mentor relationship.

more flexible working practices, mentoring has proved to be a valuable tool in managing the changed nature of an individual's work. As a consequence there is now considerable interest in books, papers and articles about mentoring. Although there is little new about the nature of mentor support, what has changed is its recognition as a legitimate and visible feature of many organizations.

Ideas about the most useful features of mentoring were offered by Kramm (1985). He emphasized the essential importance of support for the successful implementation of a scheme, and also gave some personal qualities and roles required by successful mentors. The following suggested roles and qualities expand on these.

A successful mentor should be someone interested in being a mentor, who has some stimulating ideas, and at the same time is interested in discussing other peoples' idea. In essence the most useful people to act as mentors are those with skills to exchange, those who are supportive of change in the personal, institutional, educational sense, and are able to adapt to change in time to influence and control future developments. They need to be able and willing to give time to the relationship to allow it to develop. The most successful are ready to share concerns with other mentors, to act as a coach rather than a counsellor, being open, inspiring trust and confidentiality, and encouraging, helping mentees to value their own work and development.

Other qualities found to be useful in fulfilling the task are being focused in approach, sharing clear aims, goals or objectives, being able to inspire confidence, deserving but not demanding respect and being able to cut bureaucracy where there are no adverse consequences. Such qualities were found to engender mutual respect in the mentoring relationship.

As well as personal qualities, the mentor should be in a position to influence the leadership of the department, school, college or the whole university. They would usually be in a position which is senior in some respect to the mentee, but not a direct line manager to the mentee. Again they need to be secure in status.

Recommendations for the design of an effective mentoring scheme are that there should be direct involvement of senior management, who may be able to act as role models in the scheme. Training needs to be provided both for mentors and mentees, and there should be clear management structures for directing the scheme. The scheme should be reviewed and evaluated regularly, and monitored in ways that allow the tangible benefits to be identified and valued. It should be well understood within the institution, so that all staff feel a sense of ownership of the linked successes.

Not all the possible requirements expected of a good mentor can usually be achieved in one person. It is sufficient to identify someone who is willing to learn those skills they do not already possess. Mentoring is quite separate from appraisal and assessment. A mentor is someone who is outside the system of management supervision, someone who can develop a relaxed relationship with the person being mentored. An advantage of this separation is that it allows a high degree of trust to develop between the two people directly involved. It also makes open the fact that mentoring is not just management in disguise, and it allows access to a wider range of significant contacts in the workplace than would otherwise be the case for the person being mentored.

Good mentors should be influential people who can offer significant help to mentees to reach their major life goals. They can also help reduce the isolation of a new job if they are good networkers. Mentors should be good nurturers; they should be interested in the professional development of others, and be willing to give energy to the progress of others, while respecting the prior learning of a mentee. Perhaps the most important requirements of good mentors are that they are enthusiasts who have already begun to relate their own jobs to the needs of the institution, have experience of different levels of work and have already developed active approaches to learning, drawing on a wide range of sources.

The most effective mentors are thinkers who continually question how the unit they are working in relates to the mission of the school, are still learning, keen to develop professionally and are interested in the differences between doing and understanding. Such people provide the climate that is a vital part of any learning organization (Hoy and Race, 1996).

The Role of the Critical Friend

This complements that of the mentor in respect to the relationship aspects. The critical friend is a friend who has the job of being critical in their support for the developments that are being undertaken, takes on the role of devil's advocate where necessary and points to inconsistencies overtly and directly. In contrast the mentor will help to guide the learner by listening to the mentee and by guiding through questioning them and their approach.

There is a sense in which the mentor plays more of a paternalistic role than the critical friend. Furthermore, the role of mentor fits within an organization, while the critical friend is effective from outside. The critical friend asks questions about the processes and procedures in order to clarify the issues. The mentor encourages the mentee to clarify their thinking about the processes in which they are both involved.

Wilcox and Gray (1996) outlined an important aspect of the roles of inspectors and advisers as that of 'interactive communicator', negotiating agreed definitions and purposes of activities with the people involved. This is the role played by the critical friend. As Handy (1989) has stated: 'A learning organization needs to have a formal way of asking questions, seeking out theories, testing them and reflecting upon them.'

An essential part of this process is the professional from outside the organization. The fresh eye within a relationship of trust can lead to illumination after joint reflection. This approach is well illustrated by the concept of 'portraiture' (Lightfoot, 1983). A picture of a school painted in words can provide a school with a perspective upon which to reflect before designing their action plan.

We would agree that sustainable staff development can be set in place by arranging mentors for new members of staff while using critical friends to ensure that development continues. Bearing in mind that we only make ourselves vulnerable to those whom we trust, it is vital to ensure that the roles of both mentors and critical friends are defined, and those carrying them out are carefully selected and trained. Above all a school climate has to evolve in which 'a thousand flowers bloom' and in which teachers are fully committed to continuous professional development. Resources currently used for external quality assurance will be needed to enhance opportunities for individual professional development.

The development review process in any organization must involve all members of that organization if quality is to be enhanced. The review discussion should be built into everyone's routine. All teachers and lecturers should be learning as they teach. The key to such continuous learning is the ability to ask questions. This activity is surely at the heart of learning, teaching and quality. Assessment can be used to help teachers alter classroom practice rather than simply document the practices carried out in the classroom (Gardner, 1993). The satisfaction of being involved in an organization where all are involved in seeking to improve the quality of the process will bring its own reward. We argue that this will be developed by people working together in an open climate rather than by external fiat.

The purpose of the development review process is to provide better learning for all group members in their attempts to enhance quality improvement. The desire to improve quality will determine the success of different approaches to development review. This desire can be nurtured and developed by people who are good listeners, who are patient and tolerant and who more readily ask rather than tell. Colleagues are enabled to take risks in the interests of learning, and are given space in which to try out their own ideas. Rigour can be provided by the teacher acting as researcher. As Donald Schon (1983) pointed out:

> Where teachers are encouraged to reflect-in-action, the meaning of 'good teaching' and 'a good classroom' would become topics of urgent institutional concern. Such questions could no longer be dismissed by reference to objective measures of performance. Indeed, a major question would hinge on the relationship between such measures and the qualitative judgements of individual teachers.

The major problem facing any organization that seeks to improve quality through the development review process is the temptation to overorganize. The detail and bureaucratic paperwork weigh the initiative down, and it shudders to a halt. In the same way, schools suffer from post-OFSTED exhaustion after the huge efforts necessary to meet the demands of the inspection team. As Jack Dunham (1995) has pointed out, any organization serious about professional training and development must provide a 'sharing–learning culture'. This will take time and sensitive management. The search for a method of improving quality continually, using development review and involving all staff, is addressed in Chapter 8.

4 Development From Within

There is evidence from official safety reports following serious accidents at work, such as the Piper Alpha disaster, that a reliance on external inspection creates a climate in which people feel that they are not trusted and so lose pride in their work. In schools and colleges, such reliance upon external inspection has led in many places to resentment and sometimes to dread. The determination is to beat the inspectors at their own game. The enemy at the gate drives the defenders together and does not naturally lead to a careful consideration of that which is being defended. The problem of how best to encourage schools and colleges to develop quality from within is a difficult one to tackle. Lateral thinking can be vital in the sense described by Edward de Bono (1970): 'vertical thinking is digging the same hole deeper. Lateral thinking is trying again elsewhere.'

As we saw in Chapter 2, 'inspection' is a portmanteau word, one which contains more than one meaning. Gareth Morgan (1986) has written of the power of image and metaphor in broadening our understanding of complex processes, such as inspection, which have a spectrum of meaning. At one end of the spectrum lies the military model of an external audit that checks on the smartness and effectiveness of routines. At the other end of the spectrum is the medical model in which inspection is used to diagnose ills and then suggest and even provide cures. There is, of course, another model between these two that actively involves an organization in the process by using the 'critical friend'. Critical friendships have been described as 'practical partnerships entered into voluntarily, based on relationships between equals and rooted in a common task or shared concern' (Day *et. al*, 1990). This model of inspection, which we described in Chapter 3, involves the school as an equal partner and encourages development rooted in the organization.

Inspection has triggered thinking about quality and improvement, but the audit model used by OFSTED will not of itself bring about school improvement. Indeed, it is likely to create a barrier to the commitment of the school community – headteacher, teachers, governors, parents and pupils – to managing their own school improvement. The focus has been on meeting the requirements of the inspection team and, as Ted Wragg and Tim Brighouse (1995) point out, 'implicit within it is the assumption that improvement is brought about by shaming teachers'.

It may well be argued that a national shock was needed to generate serious thinking about quality and planned school development. However, now that the national kick-start to school review and development has been delivered by OFSTED – the four-year cycle of inspection of secondary schools was completed by September 1997 – the time has come, as de Bono would say, to dig a hole elsewhere. The purpose of this would be to encourage schools to manage their own review and development in the never-ending search for quality teaching and learning.

The Deming Cycle (Neave, 1990), developed from the Shewhart Cycle of 1939 and illustrated in Figure 4.1, outlines simply the dynamic process of learning within an organization.

Any organization will benefit from developing a climate in which the process of teaching and learning is planned and checked. As the resource pack 'Quality Development', produced by Birmingham City Council Education Department (Birmingham City Council, 1992), states:

> Quality Development is essentially a process. It is a strategy, a 'way of working' that facilitates change and supports development. Quality Development makes a difference to learning and teaching by providing the stimulus and practical support for colleagues to build monitoring and evaluation into their work.

The process is rooted in the classroom. The teacher manages teaching and learning, and improvement must involve the teacher's engagement in the process. Figure 4.2 illustrates the way in which the teacher manages teaching and learning while reacting to outside influences.

The arrows indicate the way in which the teacher, at classroom level, interacts directly with outside influences. The national community only has influence upon the classroom teacher through the filter of the school, while the community does have a direct influence upon the classroom through the pupils. Above all, the influence upon the classroom is from within the school. If teachers are to learn from experience and do more than fix the system by repairing bits rather than redesigning the whole, then the focus must be on the main task of improving the quality of teaching and learning. Such an approach demands that more is done than simply rearranging the chairs on the deck of a sinking ship.

Michael Fullan (Fullan with Stiegelbanner, 1991) has written powerfully on the importance of managing change while entering into the change process oneself. He has outlined ten assumptions about change. Of these ten 'do' and 'don't' assumptions, two – numbers 2 and 10 – are particularly valuable for schools seeking to manage change from within:

Development From Within

2   Assume that any significant innovation, if it is to result in change, requires individual implementors to work out their own meaning. Significant change involves a certain amount of ambiguity, ambivalence and uncertainty for the individual about the meaning of the change. Thus, effective implementation is a process of clarification.
10 Assume that changing the culture of institutions is the real agenda, not implementing single innovations. Put another way, when implementing particular innovations we should always pay attention to whether the institution is developing or not.

The management of change is carried out against four main insights also described by Fullan:

1   Active initiation and participation
2   Pressure and support

Figure 4.1   The dynamic process of learning

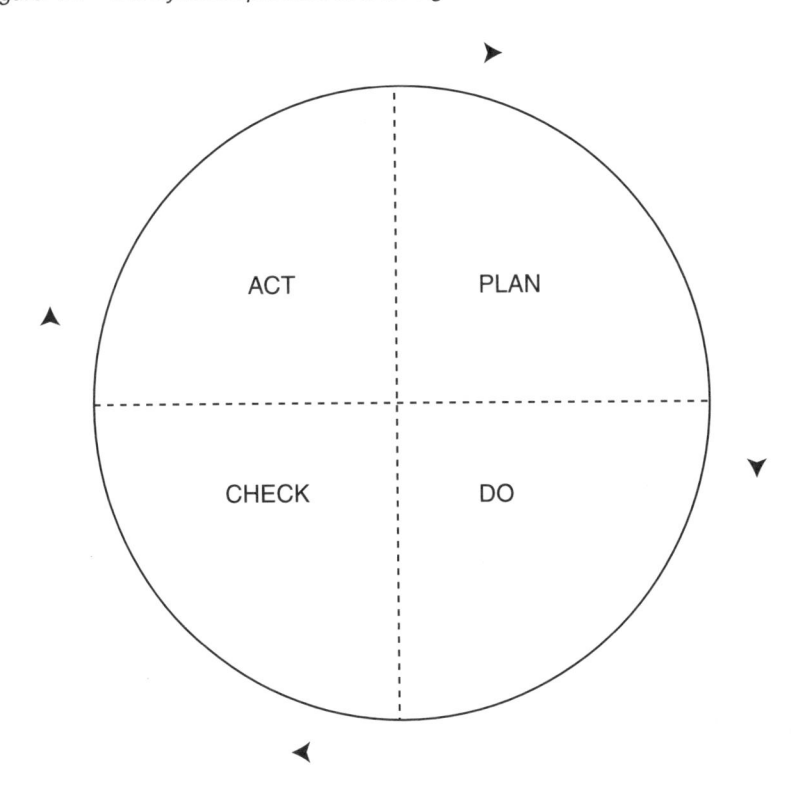

```
              ACT  │  PLAN
             ──────┼──────
             CHECK │  DO
```

Source: After Neave, 1990. Used with the permission of SPC Press, Inc., Knoxville, Tennessee

51

Development From Within

Figure 4.2 Focus for school development

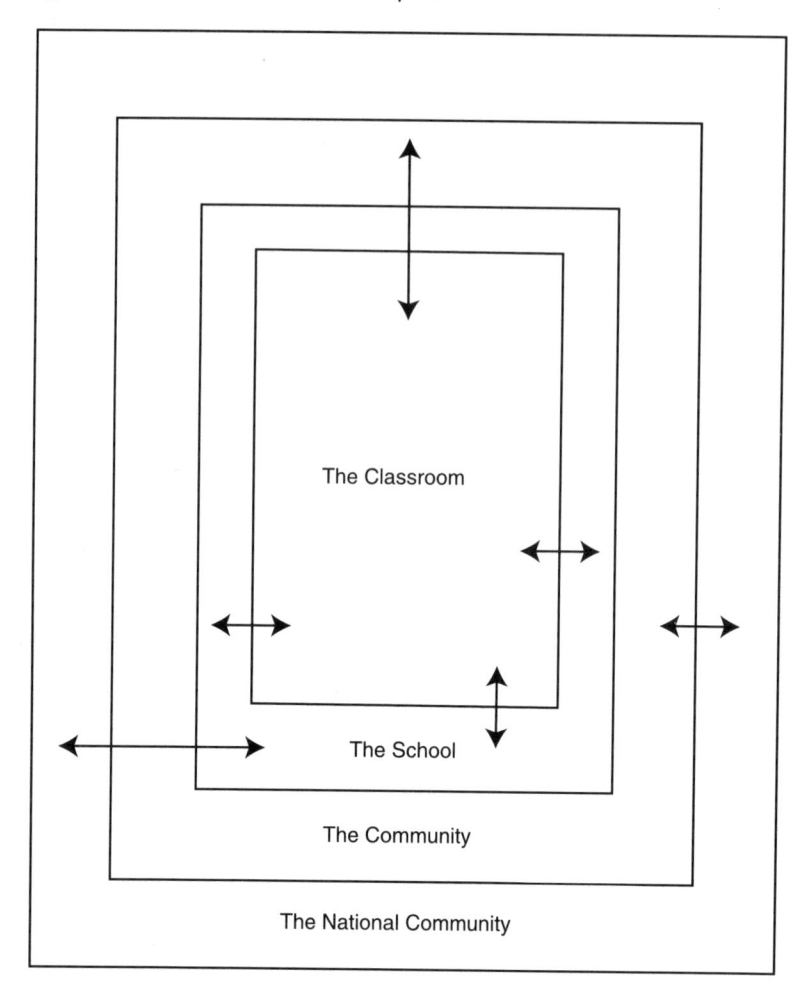

```
The Classroom
The School
The Community
The National Community
```

3   Changes in behaviour and beliefs; and
4   The overriding problem of ownership

    The process of change is not neat and linear. It is, rather, interactive and confused. Not only does a human organization change and develop internally, but outside pressures shift and change too. To manage such a process requires the ability to envisage something new and make it work. The sharing of the new ideas is, of course, an essential part of the process.
    Rosabeth Moss Kanter (1991) has identified the phases in which 'change masters' work. First, a vision is formulated and sold. Next, power is tapped to advance the ideas; and finally, the momentum has to be maintained.

Kanter's research into hundreds of managers across more than half a dozen industries provided two categories of change-master skills: personal or individual skills; and interpersonal skills – how the person manages others.

These essential skills are then further defined. Three main elements are defined for the personal skills dimension: first, kaleidoscopic thinking, or the ability to take an existing array of data, phenomena or assumptions and create an entirely new pattern; second, articulation and communication of the vision – the art of leadership; third, persistence to make the development work.

In addition to these three personal or individual skills, Kanter added three interpersonal skills. These are: first, coalition building of support groups within the organization and outside of it, of a more complex nature than the one-on-one relationship building so often researched in organizational politics; second, working through teams and creating an atmosphere in which people feel autonomous and committed; and finally, sharing the credit (as Kanter puts it, everybody involved is a 'hero').

The operation of what Burns and Stalker (1961) define as an organic system of management hinges on effective communication. This is more than providing, through the distribution of paper, notification of plans, and more than meetings for the exchange of information. Individuals are positively encouraged to apply to others for information, advice and for additional effort. Differences of status and of technical prestige are suppressed, and barriers to communication founded on functional preserves, privilege or personal reserve are removed. Any member of staff can be called upon to lead a group with a defined task, working within the framework of skills outlined by Kanter.

The learning process is complex, and change can only be brought about by teachers in their own environment. 'Renewal – whether of ponds, gardens, people or institutions – is an internal process whatever the external concerns and stimulants.' (Goodlad, 1987). There is no 'quick fix', and considerable care is needed by senior management in schools to involve teachers in consideration of the quality of the teaching and learning process. The process is, however, a creative one, as long as all involved are clearly more than technicians carrying out the ideas of others (Nichols, 1983). The simultaneous adoption of tight–loose properties, regarded by Tom Peters and Bob Waterman (1983) as essential for success, is also vital. Schools must be tight about the need for quality teaching and learning, but loose about the effective ways in which this quality can be developed.

Quality has to be built into the way in which a school works. There must be a difference to learning and teaching. One strategy is to encourage colleagues to build monitoring and evaluation into their work. Hoyle (1970) has made the point that any innovation in a school has to be adopted by social systems rather than unrelated individuals if it is to take root. Schools are organizations that are skilled at the art of adopt and adapt. All too often the adaptation can so knock the corners of a new scheme that it ceases to provide material for development. An external inspection system encourages the adaptation to meet requirements rather than empowering staff to reflect upon teaching and learning strategies. The implementation of change in schools is a socially negotiated process and has implications for the host organization. Each organization will develop its own way of micropolitical negotiation, and external demands will merely ensure that the ranks close round the existing systems.

The journey towards Stevenson's Eldorado, the goal that we shall never reach though we may descry its spires against the setting sun, is an arduous one, and anybody involved in change and development must be aware that attempts to create a tidy and controlled environment will be upset by the impact of minor happenings. As Michael Crichton wrote in his novel: 'Jurassic Park will behave in an unpredictable fashion. It is an accident waiting to happen.' A sense of purpose, a clear context and continuing negotiation of role and function will make it possible for an organization to manage change. The unexpected can and will happen, and so the tight–loose dimensions are vital.

The search for quality in teaching and learning is thus best managed as near to the classroom as possible. The way it is managed must involve the teachers, as that is the only way in which their full skills can be engaged and in which they become learners themselves. The search can be lonely, and it is vital that some form of 'critical friend' is part of the process. Perceptions of what is actually happening within the organization need to be checked against the perceptions of an outsider. In order to be effective the 'critical friend' has to be trusted. Trust is vital if members of any organization are to make themselves vulnerable to an outsider (Eisner, 1985). The catalytic type of consultancy (Morris, 1988) may well provide the most effective approach to quality development. Techniques such as portraiture, developed by Sara Lawrence Lightfoot (1983) and described in Chapter 3, provide an interesting way in which a school can be helped to see itself as others see it by considering a portrait in words by a professional outsider.

There is no panacea. Every school is unique and must start from where it is in order to improve on its previous best. Tom Peters (1987) has urged managers to come to grips with a series of paradoxes, of which the twelfth is: 'Higher quality comes with few inspections.' He points out that the processes will be improved by an involved, committed, trained work force who are supported with appropriate resources and relieved of bureaucratic meddling. Schools need to be released from the weight of OFSTED now that the issue of quality teaching and learning has been raised nationally. Schools should be positively encouraged to manage their own review and development.

During George Washington's presidency of the United States of America, two members of his first cabinet provided different approaches to the way in which the new nation should develop. Alexander Hamilton, the federalist, believed in economic control and direction by the 'better sort'. Thomas Jefferson believed in a republic in which the citizens were trusted to develop a democratic society in which the liberty of the individual was paramount. The framework for external inspection is either rooted in the Hamiltonian philosophy of control and direction or in the Jeffersonian philosophy of trusting people. The answer will lie along the continuum between the two philosophies, and in a democracy there will always be debate about the appropriate procedures. For, as Maurice Holt (1987) has pointed out, education is 'par excellence' a field in which everything depends on value judgments:

> All evaluation is ultimately based on opinion; by disguising this truth with the rituals of science, whether psychological or anthropological, we deceive and confuse ourselves, and allow our attention to be diverted from the real point – the intention which underlies our activity, and the justification for it.

In the early stages of developing the new nation, Washington listened to the advice of Hamilton because he knew the importance of setting up a sound system. Once the system was in place then came the pressure to move the approach of government towards the Jeffersonian end of the continuum. Headteachers and governors of OFSTED-inspected schools have now considered their schools in the light of the inspection report made within the Framework. Action plans have been drawn up and it is now the moment to trust schools to manage their own development.

Many schools have produced sophisticated and detailed post-OFSTED action plans. These plans and their implementation will provide the evidence as to whether or not the OFSTED inspection brings about development. The most interesting plans and those most likely to have an impact are those made with governors, parents and teachers involved. The key to development in any organization is to harness the energy of those within, using the skills of vision-building outlined by Kanter (1991). The exact process must be a matter for each organization. It is not a matter of painting by numbers.

In further and higher education the basic work of learning and teaching in the classroom, laboratory and lecture hall depends, just as in the school classroom, upon the element of trust – trust between the students and their teachers, and between the college or university department and its management body. This is particularly true in relation to managing their own resources. The interaction between practitioners and outside influences needs to be based upon the classroom focus – learning from experience, for the task of improving the quality of learning starts with the task of managing the change improvement process.

What has the government done to help this take effect? They have given to the Quality Assurance Agency the task of putting into a coherent whole the systems for identifying and ensuring standards in higher education, as the response to the Dearing and Garrick Reports suggest. By March 1998, the agency had published its consultative paper, 'An Agenda for Quality', the title of which was a throwback to the Manpower Services Commission title, 'An Agenda for Action for the Youth Training Scheme' of some twenty years earlier. Standards, we maintain, are the scales against which quality is measurable. In crude terms they are like the revs/mph in top gear of a car. This is a universe away from the skills needed to design and build an engine to perform to some such set limit.

The Quality Assurance Agency offerings were based upon a complex of interlocking proposals (Tysome, 1998) as parts of a new system. In the light of comments made by such interested parties as the Committee of Vice Chancellors and Principals, the employers' organizations and the Association of University Teachers, these proposals were rethought in May 1998, but they still overlooked a fundamental issue, the quality of the student learning experience.

Such a complicated structure misses entirely the focus of the quality element which rests with the teachers themselves. The 1998 system envisaged six elements in the array of quality assurance, ranging from more exacting statements of course content to examining practices and the actual award of degree qualifications themselves. These have little to do directly with the quality of the student learning experience. What they address instead is the mechanics of checking – checking that what the central authorities deem to be quality, i.e. conformity to set rules, is being followed exactly. Precise outcomes replace learning, and education becomes training.

The structure envisaged the need to tighten up on qualifications. It also saw a need for institutions to offer clearer descriptions of the content and aims of their courses. So-called benchmarking was to be introduced, based upon the abilities and attributes expected of graduates. These would differ from subject to subject, and allowed that they may also focus on curriculum, if professional bodies involved in these fields agreed. Standards were to be checked in forty-one different subject areas, and there was to be a new role for external examiners. Defined threshold standards were seen as the minimum necessary for the award of a degree. At that time the plans envisaged 'registered external examiners'– again implying conformity to some approved/external standard – who would use guides written by 'benchmarking groups' for each subject to check and compare standards.

The emphasis on standards again misses the point that it is the goodwill of the lecturing staff that determines the quality of the learning taking place. Any number of set standards can be invented, yet the proof of the learning in attitude, ability or aptitude enhancement will be the product of the learning process.

Development From Within

In more detail, the 1998 proposed Standards in Higher Education were as follows:

1. *Qualifications*: a new National Higher Education Qualification was proposed, based on the Dearing Report's recommendation of eight levels from Higher National Certificate and Higher National Diploma to Higher Education Certificate and National Vocational Qualification (NVQ) level 3, up to doctorate and NVQ level 5.
2. *Templates*: institutions were to be required to provide students, employers and quality councils with clearer descriptions of the content and aims of their courses.
3. *Benchmarking*: the Dearing and Garrick Reports proposed that standards should be more clearly defined. The Quality Assurance Agency suggested that these should be in terms of the abilities and attributes expected of graduates – differing subject by subject – but allowed that they may also focus on curriculum if professional bodies involved in these fields agreed. Threshold standards were to be seen as the minimum necessary, and there were plans to have registered external examiners who would use guides written by benchmarking groups for each subject to check and compare standards.
4. *Subject Areas*: the Quality Assurance Agency drew up a list of forty-one different subject areas on which standards were to be checked, and the Agency also set out guidelines for the knowledge base that graduates should possess and be able to demonstrate at the end of their degree course.
5. *External Examiners*: the original proposals were that Institutions should propose two or more examiners in each subject area who would report to the Quality Assurance Agency as registered external examiners. Their job would have been to check standards and level of an award, to see that course objectives were being achieved. They would consider curriculum design and content, students' learning experience, assessment and resources.

Problems were anticipated, as these proposals envisaged major changes to practices followed at that time, so variations were almost immediately suggested. Ideas being considered would have:

- External Examiners reporting to institutions on standards, as they traditionally have done, with the Quality Assurance Agency getting copies of their reports.
- Academic Reviewers, appointed by the Quality Assurance Agency, working with institutional review teams to scrutinize course quality. The reviewers would work closely with the external examiners, so there would be no need for an external subject review team.

6 *Codes of Practice*: this is the proposal which would see the Quality Assurance Agency writing standard Codes of Practice that institutions would have to follow in line with the Dearing and Garrick proposals. These were to cover quality assurance, public information and standards, student support and guidance, overseas students, collaborative work and post-graduate work. It was envisaged that the codes would be universally valid and applicable by focusing on results, rather than on how these results were achieved. How the codes were applied in individual institutions was to be monitored every five or six years. The minimum expectations were set out in a draft code issued in the summer of 1998. Reviews were envisaged to cover three areas:

- Degree Awarding – through an audit of a university's arrangements for the award of its degrees.
- Good Practice – through a checking process to ensure that institutions had in place arrangements to verify outcomes of their codes of practice. These were to be assessed as appropriate, inadequate or exemplary.
- Quality of Teaching and Learning – through a university's own system of quality assurance, checked by the Quality Assurance Agency. The outcome would be a measure of the effectiveness of an institution's own processes against external accountability.

In cases where an institution was 'below par', an assessment of that institution, or of some subject areas, might then have to be contemplated. The debate was not concluded by the end of 1998, and expectations were that there would still be discussions on the effects in practice for some time to come. However, it is another indication of the extent to which conformity to patterns being set by central government is influencing the inspection process itself.

The evidence from government involvement in quality assurance at all levels of education is that the audit approach dominates. Standards are set within frameworks, and there is scant sensitivity to the process within an organization by which quality development takes place. There is growing recognition of this, and in the booklet 'Improving Schools' (HMSO, 1994), OFSTED conceded that there is no single answer to school improvement. The booklet begins: 'There is no single route to the improvement of schools, nor any single point on a school's route to improvement at which it can stop and call the process complete.'

One route to unlocking the potential for improving quality that lies within a school through a productive partnership is outlined in Chapter 6. The emphasis must be on the partnership, and the ownership of the process remains with the school. Essentially the school is learning, and questions from 'critical friends' have a positive impact if they are open. Questions that seek to lead the learner to a particular solution and are closed will not encourage the school to own its development. The 'Quality Development Resource Pack' produced by Birmingham City Council (1992) is another example of a partnership approach to development from within. This impressive resource pack covers the rationale and the process of quality development as experienced in Birmingham, and is genuine in that it does not prescribe a particular route. In the section 'School – Know Thyself!' (p. 66), schools are encouraged to engage in some self-reflection early on to prepare the ground and inform any decision about action research that might be undertaken. The open nature of the approach by the LEA is shown in this section:

> You may be asking, 'Why not wait until after training?' Here is another example of the need for differentiation between schools according to the circumstances of the individual institution. For some institutions it may be helpful to involve the whole staff in this degree of reflection prior to choosing a coordinator, for others this may be regarded as high risk or likely to stifle the initiative....This activity may benefit from the support of an external party who is known and trusted by the school.
> (Birmingham City Council, 1992)

Teachers in schools deserve our respect, as they are working within an organization to educate others. Partnership can encourage development from within, whereas directions from outside simply stifle growth by destroying the sense of ownership of the process within the institution in the interests of regimentation.

Teaching is essentially a busy and demanding activity. It is vital that, in letting go the reins of central control, there is no attempt to overorganize the Jeffersonian approach to school review and development. According to Senge (1990), learning must be a lifelong process. Teachers must always be in the state of practising the disciplines of learning, and Weick (1985) has likened the process to surfing on waves of events and decisions. Nobody can ride the surf successfully to detailed instructions from the shore.

5 Validated Self-Review
Towards a Working Model

Validated Self-Review and Quality Development

Validated self-review can be a powerful and effective mechanism for quality development, harnessing the internal capability of the institution for self-development and self-renewal. At the same time it increases the capacity for redefinition and regeneration. This is the evolutionary paradigm, the pattern for renewal and rebirth. Quality which fails to evolve and reinvent itself becomes endangered. There are parallels in selective breeding, improvement through development of the best quality while inferior quality withers away. Validated self-review is inherently synergistic. It works through cooperation and partnership, the operation of an alliance for quality in which the partners have complementary roles to play, combining their efforts in pursuit of a shared goal. The goal is the enhancement of best practice and the eradication of poor quality which constrains learning potential. (See Deming's view outlined in the Introduction.)

As organizations in the post-industrial world seek competitive advantage through the development of people and exploitation of information, the pursuit of quality and continuous improvement has become an important aim in both private and public sectors.

The Business Excellence model, developed by the European Foundation for Quality Management and the British Quality Foundation, is being used increasingly by organizations. It provides a rigorous and externally validated process for assessment of an organization's processes and results. Originally developed in the private sector, the requirement to demonstrate best value in services has increased the use of the model in the public sector, including educational organizations. OFSTED, in its publication *School Evaluation Matters* (DfEE, 1998b), recommends that schools adapt the model as a mechanism for validated self-review.

The model focuses on two key areas of organizational life: enablers, which describes those key processes for organizational success; and results, which concentrates on measures of organizational performance.

Each of these areas is divided into criteria as follows:

Validated Self-Review

Enablers
- Leadership
- Policy and strategy
- People management
- Management of resources
- Processes

Results
- Customer satisfaction
- People satisfaction
- Impact on society
- Business results (financial and non-financial)

In an organizational assessment, evidence is gathered across the organization according to guidance supplied by the British Quality Foundation. A scoring system is then applied to score each criterion. These are weighted, customer satisfaction being given the highest single weighting, with people management and people satisfaction combined having the second highest weighting.

When assessed and scored against the model, organizations can be confident about a sound and externally validated measure of organizational performance, and the generation of valuable information and ideas on organizational strengths and areas for improvement.

However, there are certain shortcomings of such validated self-review. One significant potential shortcoming is the need for schools to have gained sufficient expertise in the skills needed to engage in this process effectively. Another is central government's mistrust of school self-review being sufficiently rigorous. The 'rose-coloured spectacles' syndrome is indeed a potential pitfall, but requires some form of validation. Unfortunately the 'validation' provided by OFSTED lacks a close contextual knowledge built up over time. It seems to us that proper, rigorous validation must take into account the individual school context much more than the OFSTED model permits. To this end the validated self-review is a valued alternative to the current OFSTED model of external inspection against a framework.

The self-review process requires mastery of certain key capabilities:

- a capacity for critical self reflection
- frank and honest appraisal of areas of expertise and limitations
- the development of a climate of trust
- an openness to constructive comment whereby colleagues feel sufficiently secure, professionally, to expose their methods, as practitioners, to the scrutiny of others as part of peer review of practice

Validated Self-Review

These key capabilities define a 'quality enhancing' culture, one of the distinguishing characteristics of schools as learning communities. It is energized and renewed through its own internally generated quest for excellence, and its intolerance of deficiencies and mediocrity. It is a culture which is both idealistic and practical, having a vision of perfection but aware of practicalities and constraints. It guards against the dangers of insularity by engaging in wider debates and working with external partners sharing the same commitment to continuous improvement. An objective external assessment of strengths and areas for development can serve as a stimulus to improvement through validating the school's own self-scrutiny and affirming best practice, thus enhancing confidence and stimulating further development. However, such review must be sufficiently rigorous to challenge weaker aspects and to call the school to account for its own actions.

A Partnership for Quality

This chapter draws upon the experience of one Local Education Authority (LEA) which has established a partnership for quality development at local level with its schools through the operation of its own agreed model of validated self-review. This LEA has launched and is operating very successful school improvement projects across schools in the borough. The discussion is broadened to consider an 'alliance for quality' based on LEA support for school review, and provides additional context to the study in Chapter 6. The LEA reassesses, refines and adapts its role, in common with other LEAs in recent years, but its commitment to the development of a quality enhancing culture has remained one of its core purposes.

The days which saw the LEA as an unyielding, inflexible, rigid enforcer of education at local level are long gone. The LEA role is now defined more keenly in terms of a strategic partner working with schools, influencing and shaping the culture at local level. In many different ways the LEA's work can add value to the work of schools, by affirming what is good, stimulating development and enhancing capability to improve weaker practice. The LEA can use its wider knowledge across its schools to put them in touch with one another, and so promote networks at local level where teachers and schools are helped to draw on one another's experiences, share expertise and develop collegially. This aspect of a quality enhancing culture militates against the divisive effects of competitiveness and the operation of market forces which can set school against school and so deny possibilities for shared learning and working together. The process of validating school self-review facilitates the strategic role of the LEA by providing the information needed to form a view of quality across schools.

LEAs have a close knowledge of their schools, built up over time, which helps in target setting with schools. They also have an understanding of local politics and a role in informing the policy decisions of the local

Validated Self-Review

council. This particular LEA has a great deal of expertise, upon which schools frequently draw to inform planning, enhance skills and capabilities, and to seek an outside view of standards and quality. The LEA recognizes that the prime responsibility for quality development lies with schools themselves but an effective system of validated self-review can be a powerful force for improvement. If insufficiently rigorous it can be open to challenge and accusations of being a too cosy arrangement which lacks a hard edge. Thus difficult messages that may sometimes need to be delivered remain unspoken. The challenge is to achieve the right balance between affirming and celebrating excellence, and confronting poor quality.

The balance can be a difficult one to strike. Hard messages are sometimes needed, and these are arguably more likely to be heeded and acted upon when delivered by someone for whom the school has respect. With a close knowledge of the individual context, built up over time, LEAs are far better placed than a team of inspectors hitherto unknown to the school when it comes to relevant plans. The views and judgments of the latter may well be regarded as no more than a snapshot, based upon a three- or four-day visit rather than on a close knowledge which has unfolded through a relationship sustained across a number of years. It will hold less meaning for the school than the judgments of a respected partner. However, as we have stated before, the LEA needs to act as critical friend, at times being 'robustly challenging' (DfEE, 1998a) in the messages it delivers and the degree of rigour it imparts to schools. Particular skills are required for the role of the critical friend, and LEA advisers require training to meet the challenge of a changing scene.

The 'snapshot' approach has the power of statute to ensure that the messages and findings are followed up, but whether this is an effective model for the development of enduring quality improvements is being questioned. To have the power to endure, to take root and grow, there must be commitment to the outcomes through 'ownership' of the processes. A school's motivation to achieve will be sapped and weakened if schools are left with the abiding feeling that their situation has not been fully understood.

Staff, who are neither engaged as professional partners in dialogue nor given a share in building frameworks for development, lose the energy and interest to effect sustained quality improvements. As Deming so powerfully argued, people must feel involved in a process so that they seek to build in quality all the time. Those who are working to an external agenda, in which they feel they have no say, are unlikely to commit themselves with energy and enthusiasm to the enterprise.

Correctly applied, the philosophy of validated self-review respects the right to self-determination. By centring improvement within the institution itself, development teams are empowered to take the reins of the improvement processes. A capacity for critical self-awareness is fostered. The self-review methodology involves systematic stocktaking, and this must have resonance with the process of taking forward the attainment of the core purposes of teaching and learning. The validation comes through a second pair of eyes, a critical friend. Such scrutiny may both confirm the school's own self examination and provide a spur to enhancing learning. The prerequisite is that practice is opened up to questioning and close examination, together with a willingness to revisit previous assumptions and ways of working when challenged to do so.

The LEA in question operates a 'Framework for Supporting School Self Review', which has been agreed with the schools. The Framework has two important purposes:

> to help schools to take a systematic approach to the review and evaluation of their relative strengths and weaknesses; and to support and strengthen the relationship between schools and the LEA in working together to raise standards and develop and improve quality.

This embodies the philosophy of an 'alliance for quality', with the LEA and schools agreed on a core mission and combining their efforts to make a difference for children. The schools ask themselves the question, 'How well are we doing?', as the starting point for a process of stocktaking, and this process and its outcomes, in terms of planned actions for improvement, are supported and guided by complementary LEA expertise and assistance. This is part of the LEA's proactive role in helping to make a difference through engaging schools in assessing their own performance and contributing to that assessment through external endorsement. As this book has stated many times already and in a number of different ways, at its core is the belief that an effective strategy for quality development is internally motivated rather than externally driven. A key task for the LEA adviser is to make a major contribution towards the improvement in quality of education in schools, and the Self-Review Framework provides a means within which to accomplish this purpose:

> 'How well are we doing?' is a structure of support for the LEA and its schools to work together to gain a clear understanding of the improvements that have been made in attainment and quality.
> (LEA document, 'Validating School Improvement Through School Review')

To repeat, the best critical friend enjoys the trust and respect of schools. The critical friend must be seen to understand each school's own distinctive situation and circumstances, its ambitions and ideals. In strengthening a self-developing quality culture, the critical friend is not simply there to ratify and commend but also to challenge assumptions, stimulate debate and promote an enhanced capacity for reflection. The critical friend plays a part in

Validated Self-Review

enhancing necessary expertise and competence through skills training, advice and consultancy to maximize the capabilities of the school team, and thereby stimulate the improvement effort. The critical friend needs a close and careful understanding of the characteristics of the individual setting.

We believe that the LEA in question puts into practice the theme of this book, namely that quality development is most effective when it is located within the schools themselves, and that self-review is an important mechanism by which the self-determining school gains in self knowledge and regulates its functions in order to maximize effectiveness. The role of the LEA in validating this internal process has many important by-products. One of these has been to create the habit, in staffrooms and classrooms, of teachers talking about and reflecting critically on practice in informed and considered ways. Stimulating this reflective dialogue is an important part of the improvement process, encouraging teachers to share their thought and practice both within their schools and with other schools. It also assists them to experiment, analyse, observe and critically examine the dictum that 'we do it like this because it has always been done this way'. How hard it is to forsake custom and practice and to come to the view that tradition may not be the most educationally sound rationale for perpetuation of current practice! Improvement needs to go hand-in-hand with a desire to change. Sometimes this can create feelings of vulnerability and therefore, unsurprisingly, a certain defensiveness. Stimulating dialogue among teachers about their professional practice and the structures and frameworks within which they operate helps the improvement process.

The process then gains its own internally driven momentum, rather than one brought about by an outside force. This stocktaking can necessarily be a heart-searching procedure demanding an honest appraisal of 'where are we now?', before formulating strategies to take us to where we realistically wish to be. Improving quality in education can be a painful process. Honestly placing one's practice under the spotlight can, on the one hand, illuminate our successes and strengths which we may wish to expose to others, but it necessarily also involves displaying weaknesses and limitations. An important consideration for school leaders is how to strengthen a culture in which the spotlight can sharpen our understanding without creating threat or nostalgia for how things used to be, or defensiveness and a sense of vulnerability each of which undermines energy and impedes development.

The role of critical friend is an extremely demanding one. It involves providing many different functions, for example, the critical friend must be considered and thorough, discerning and challenging, but at the right level for each school. Too much challenge can be disabling. They need to be well informed, both in respect of the distinctiveness of each school setting and in the sense of their own understanding of current issues and debates about quality and improvement locally and nationally. Other skills are needed in guiding and supporting each school's efforts; and, most importantly, the critical friend needs to be a valued, respected and trusted colleague.

In this particular case (see Chapter 6) the LEA has designated link advisers for each school, and it is their task to provide another pair of eyes to look at the internally generated process. The school becomes an organization that learns while improving learning within itself.

This learning can be extended and deepened through the validation process, and important skills and competencies gained. These advance the capacity of the school to effect improvement. Part of the process of improving quality is having a closer understanding about how we learn. In this way we become more effective in teaching in ways which achieve a closer correspondence with how learning takes place to maximize learning gains:

> If learning is the most important outcome of what happens in schools, then teaching is the principal means by which this learning is brought about. And teaching – what teachers do, how they teach – is shaped primarily by what they believe about learning and about learners, rather than by what they are told to do by any textbook or course description.
> (Scottish CCC, 1996), p. iii)

The process of self-review is essentially one of self-learning. The LEA injects rigour and challenge into this process as a spur to further improvement. Challenging a 'cruising' or 'coasting' school to question assumptions and ways of working, and so arouse it from complacency, is a necessary role for the LEA to engage with the school self-review process, prompting the quest for enhanced quality:

> There are many examples of good practice, where LEAs have worked hard to develop a relationship with their schools ... and which is securing high and improving standards. In such cases the LEA has earned the respect of schools for its leadership, for the quality of the advice and services it provides, and for an approach which is always supportive while being robustly challenging when needed. Schools welcome the LEA's involvement, and value close partnership and frequent contact, without abrogating responsibility for their own performance. Where such relationships already exist and are delivering excellence, they are a testament to the skill and commitment of both LEA and schools.
> (DfEE, 1998a, paragraph 6, pp. 3–4)

Self-Review in Higher and Further Education

It is interesting to note that developments in this sector provide another example of the move towards validated self-review. Teaching delivery in universities and colleges is currently assessed against what the institution sets as out in its documentation as its targets on delivery.

The core documentation presented by the institution is the Self-Assessment Document (SAD) with its foundation of aims and objectives for each department, school, centre, course and unit. This needs to be pitched at the right level, with reasonable claims aiming at reasonable standards of delivery. There is no point in university departments setting down claims that cannot be substantiated through evidence, or documented in curriculum examples. The individual modules and units of the course need to demonstrate that an objective stated in the SAD is being addressed. Additionally, there must be evidence on which to assess whether that policy is being successfully provided. Feedback, in the form of comments from others such as peer groupings and external examiners, is useful here. There are also basic statements of what the institution actually does, why does it, and why it believed it to be useful. Outcomes need to be evaluated and documentation on how the issues that arise are dealt with presented and addressed. Induction, staff development and student feedback processes have a strong bearing here. Student perceptions – of the quality they receive from the system in terms of counselling, health and tutorial support – also feature alongside retention rates to assure the external bodies that there is evidence of an actively managed and consciously reflective operation.

Such a system encourages institutions to design realistic policies. The points then awarded by the visiting teams of assessors are not absolute in any way; they only reflect consistency with claimed status from individual institutions. There is no standard value attached to the numerical scoring, despite that being the implication inherent in the scoring awarded. It is merely a recognition of consistency of delivery – of doing what they say they are doing. This leaves a lot to be read into quality on the ground in the classroom and lecture halls of universities and colleges. In the current model, effective quality means consistency of output, and encourages conformity of approach. If processes and procedures are in place to deliver that, then the judgment is assured and a quality grading awarded. There is no attempt to enhance quality, to ensure that improvement is being inculcated into the institutional processes as such. That is where the external audit of the future should score heavily. That system will allow questions of procedure, or purpose or attainments past and present, and a focus on the procedures adopted to review the current status and enhancement and professional development being adopted to ensure improvement in the actions taken by all.

Proposals for revised quality assessment mechanisms for further and higher education provide another example of self-review. The model currently in use will be replaced by one relying on the self-regulation of quality from internal procedures and processes. There will still be an expectation of contact with employers to ascertain their degree of satisfaction with the outcomes of the courses – the graduates they take into employment – but this is seen as part of the accepted procedures of the institutions themselves. The need is for staff in the colleges and universities to want to be assured that they are meeting the expectations of employers of their graduates. The onus will be firmly upon university staff themselves to satisfy their own internal peer groups of their competency. The external bodies will be looking for an agreed audit of the procedures rather than carrying out the inspections themselves through a detailed assessment visit to the institution. Evidence will need to be presented and checked by an assessment body to assure the quality of the programmes offered by the university.

This process comes from a quite different philosophy of assessment to that currently imposed, with the visiting Quality Assessment group themselves finding out what the employers' views are of the material being assessed. The focus becomes one of consistency of approach, on how to build-in better teaching styles and content. Accreditation by institution, probably for a period of five years and with reviews before extension of the accreditation, appears to be the present considered view of the Quality Assurance Agency for the future. This already holds in the case of post-graduate teacher training departments in colleges and universities. The importance of peer review of teaching, mentoring schemes and the use of the critical friend will be enhanced. On-going internal questioning of processes of teaching and learning are then not a once-and-for-all, externally imposed assessment procedure. This will be a welcome approach to that imposed currently. The stigma of the 'failing school' has not been attached to universities and colleges because the process has been about subject departments and their work rather than the sum total of the university's provision. Nevertheless there have been some worrying comments about the identification of outcomes. In some cases this has resulted in appeals which have, on subsequent visits, resulted in a regrading of that department to a higher classification under the pre-1996 procedures.

In future, the focus will become one of assurance that the internal workings are being applied, that reviews of the structure of course provision are undertaken, that aims, goals, objectives and learning outcomes are being rigorously followed in the modes of assessment and examination of the candidates taking the programmes. The records of information considered from feedback mechanisms, the discussions between the teams teaching the courses, their internal and external examiners, will still need identifying. This will be undertaken in future by others within the institution – and afterwards subject to external audit. An alternative suggestion is to place subject reviewers with the internal teams as they meet to review their courses and programmes every five years. This appears to be a step towards the establishment of a continual application of a process we advocate to enhance quality. It is time consuming, yet has the potential of developing a culture looking towards improvement rather than inspection. It is to be hoped that these policy recommendations are implemented in an acceptable form to focus on the opportunity to improve, not on a labelling as 'sub-standard'. The current scoring system needs amending at the same time, since some media outlets have misused it to such an extent as to invalidate completely the barely reliable system adopted at present. In essence it is likely to produce an on-going video of developments towards improving quality in education in place of the instant photo of the set test now being applied at intervals, with the institution being primed for the inspection process well in advance. In future the institutions will have to demonstrate procedures to ensure constant and continuous improvement in quality – a much taller order indeed, and one in which all staff will be engaged on a continuing basis. Presentation becomes less important than the on-going debates between staff on the enhancing of the process. We are almost back to the HMI pattern of regular informal visits to schools, using the models abandoned in 1992.

In contrast to the current processes in place for further and higher education, the experiences retold in the on-going school case studies in Chapter 6 demonstrate the operation in practice of the notion of an 'alliance for quality' which was introduced at the beginning of this chapter. The approach to quality development is through the establishment of a 'quality enhancing culture' of self-learning and competition against oneself, with the aim of enhancing previous performance. This is ultimately more meaningful than market driven approaches to quality improvement, which are not only divisive in setting school against school, but are also flawed.

There is no standard model for the process of self-review, and this has led to a variety of attempts to validate the process. Peter Holly (1986) pointed out that professional evaluation was communicative, informative, interactive, insightful, consciousness-raising, critical and 'the antithesis of education as recitation, social control and dependency.' LEAs produced checklists against which schools could evaluate their self-review, but as John Elliott (1981) wrote, they are 'essentially an instrument for increasing technical efficiency and control rather than the capacity to make reflective professional decisions'. The Guidelines for Review and Internal Development (GRIDS) project was perhaps the major effort to provide teachers with a framework within which to evaluate teaching and learning. This project also failed to engage teachers in self-review. These efforts by external bodies to organize school review always end up by using some form of quantifiable list or framework to constrain and control schools. This is the closed approach, already mentioned in Chapter 4.

Many LEAs have learned from these attempts to help schools, and are adopting a more open-ended approach. In 1991, Hereford and Worcester LEA outlined for professional development coordinators questions that they needed to ask when planning school developments:

Deciding how to monitor progress and to judge achievements

It is important to decide at the planning stage:
- how you will recognise the achievement of your aims;
- what evidence you will need to collect to enable you to do this;
- who will monitor the progress of the plan;
- who will collect the evidence of success;
- how and to whom it will be reported;
- how you will use the information you have gathered.

(Bayne-Jardine and Holly, 1994, pp. 32–3)

By asking questions, schools were helped to set up their own process of self review. Birmingham, in its 'Quality Development Resource Pack' (1992, p. 33), takes a similar stance:

> QD in Birmingham is not a 'fixed' or 'finished' strategy for school improvement. It will continue to grow and develop, influenced by our schools' experience of putting it into practice as well as informed by lessons from elsewhere.

The spirit of inquiry is at the heart of organizational developments. This spirit of inquiry can all too easily be chained to the chariot wheels of those with agendas outside the schools. Perhaps the way in which to fuel the spirit of inquiry in any school is to ask questions and to probe with insiders their answers. Once more the critical friend provides the most effective support. In 'Out of the Crisis', Deming (1982, ch. 5) presents sixty-six questions to help managers. Many of these questions relate to the industrial world, but the model is clear and most questions can easily be transferred to the educational context. The essence of Question 66 makes this point clear: 'What are you doing about quality...?'

By asking questions, outsiders can help teachers refine the processes of teaching, learning, the curriculum and the interaction of those elements. In a real sense the outsider becomes part of the review process by questioning the practitioners so that they explain exactly what they are doing, and by so doing gain greater understanding.

Validated Self-Review in Practice: Background to Case Study

What follows in Chapter 6 is a report of a small-scale study of one Local Education Authority (LEA) which has sought to create a culture and climate to nurture and stimulate school improvement across its schools. The data is presented school by school for each sample school. It is organized in sections to highlight the important unique features of each school, discovered through interviews and discussions with staff from each school, and covers

Validated Self-Review

their perception of the contribution made by the School Improvement Projects in which they were involved. An evaluation of the improvement made to quality development in their own school is made case by case on the basis of the views of each school.

In all five schools in the study, the LEA in question has given a clear lead in the drive for improvement and has supported schools engaged in the improvement process. The role of LEAs in relation to school improvement is discussed in *Excellence in Schools* (DfEE, 1997a), and the combination of pressure and support, when applied effectively, can provide a stimulus to improvement. This LEA has offered an opportunity to schools to work in partnership, with one another and with the LEA, to strengthen good practice and to work together towards enhanced levels of success. The research for Chapter 6 has as its evidence base semi-structured interviews conducted with four primary schools (named in the study as St Andrew's Primary, Teesdale Primary, Chadwick Infants and Wideacre Primary), together with one secondary school, (Rising Dale Secondary School). The schools are real schools but their names have been changed in order to guarantee anonymity.

Other evidence comes from interviews conducted with LEA personnel, together with supporting documentation provided by these five schools and the LEA. This evidence base does not claim to be representative of all the schools under the LEA engaging in the School Improvement Projects, but instead it offers to the reader the personal accounts of a small number of schools which have actively embarked on the tasks of quality development, in partnership with the LEA. They have been willing to reflect on this process and retell their own personal accounts of participation in the LEA School Improvement Projects (SIPs). Their comments have been faithfully reported in unedited form. This allows the schools to speak for themselves, and we the authors to be true to our actual sources. The work offers some analysis of the experiences of these schools based on a consideration of their accounts in the context of wider debate about LEA support for school improvement.

The setting is a metropolitan borough in the north of England. It is a multicultural borough where approximately one-fifth of the school population comes from the growing ethnic minority communities. Many of these students have Punjabi, Bengali, Gujerati or Urdu as their first language, and are therefore learners of English as a second language. Unemployment rates, among young people in the Pakistani and Bengali communities in particular, are high.

Many of the features of social and economic disadvantage associated with areas of industrial decline and economic change are manifest in the borough. Poverty is a feature, but its incidence is not uniform and there are marked economic and social contrasts between areas of affluence and those of deprivation within its boundaries. The interaction of these factors has contributed to low levels of educational achievement as measured by some nationally recognized indicators, such as school examination results and rates of participation in post-compulsory education.

The School Improvement Projects are part of the work of the School Development Service branch of the LEA. Managing and supporting the work of these projects falls within the remit of the advisers, whose role has a clear focus on school improvement. In addition, other colleagues in the Support Services such as the Ethnic Minorities Support Service and the Special Needs Support Service also have an involvement. The projects operate through a collaborative partnership, with schools and LEA personnel working together in pursuit of raised standards of achievement and effectiveness.

The local context for quality improvement

This LEA has a tradition of collaborative partnership and shared ways of working with schools. A shared value system guides the work of the LEA in its relationships with schools, and there is a tradition of consultation with schools in decision making. Shared frameworks of understanding have been built up over time, and the SIPs must be seen as part of a culture of effective support for school improvement through partnership. Prior to the 1992 Education (Schools) Act, this LEA had operated its own review strategy of school development which was based on a commitment to promote continuous improvement within a model of validated self-review. This model for effective quality development proceeded from a shared value system which was explicit. It was agreed with schools, and grounded in a commitment to dialogue, shared and open ways of working, and was intended to make a significant contribution to the improvement of the quality of education in schools across the borough. The model was based on a respect for the autonomy of schools and the belief that schools themselves are responsible for effecting improvement. Schools, recognized as self managing and self developing communities, were encouraged to work with the LEA to define their own success targets and to evaluate their own progress towards achieving them. This was the embodiment of a philosophy aimed at harnessing a spirit of self-determination in schools. The role of the LEA was to support progress towards the specified goals of the School Development Plan and provide a wider external perspective. The LEA therefore operated using link advisers in the role of 'critical friend', offering a validation of each school's own self scrutiny, sometimes asking hard questions where necessary, perhaps challenging a school to look again at an aspect of its practice, and offering advice and consultancy as necessary.

This new model, while grounded in the same philosophy, has been redefined to embrace a keener focus on school improvement. The current approach to LEA-validated self review is set out in a series of phase-specific booklets which were produced by a working group, the membership of which included headteachers, advisers and officers. The substance of the booklets was the subject of a wide consultative process carried out with schools within the LEA. The focus of the strategy is LEA validation of school improvement through school self-review. One of its principles is that it should support and integrate with school improvement strategies and with monitoring, advice and support for schools. In other words, the initiative, ownership and direction belong to the schools. The LEA takes the role of the critical friend.

The School Improvement Projects (SIPs)

In 1995/96 the LEA launched the first round of SIPs. These covered a number of different topics, and schools opted-in on a voluntary basis, often selecting the topic which would meet School Development Plan targets or those targets arising from the post-OFSTED action plan. The SIPs have been offered in each subsequent year and have had a clear focus on raising achievement. SIP themes have included: effective curriculum management; continuity and progression; effective teaching; improving standards in literacy; improving standards in numeracy; monitoring pupil progress; and raising the achievement of boys. Some of the SIPs have been focused on the primary phase while other project areas have operated in the secondary phase. Levels of school participation have been high, and many schools have renewed their involvement from one year to the next.

The process

The SIP process begins with a School Action Plan, which is usually drawn up by the school's senior management and staff from the School Development Service (SDS) working together. This is a crucial part of the SIP process, as the action plan enshrines the specific focus of the SIP in the school and the school targets to be met during the course of the project. It embodies the targets for improvement, the strategies by which they are to be realised and the criteria for monitoring and evaluating success.

As the project proceeds in the school, guidance and advice is provided by the LEA as appropriate for each school's needs. Each SIP is initially for one year's duration, and in the final stages the school reviews and assesses the extent to which the action plan targets have been realized. This final review is normally supported by SDS personnel.

The SDS arranges a conference each year in the summer term to launch the SIPs and a conference in the autumn term to support the progress of the SIPs in participating schools. In addition, dissemination conferences, newsletters and regular network meetings are held. Speakers of national standing are invited to give keynote addresses at the conferences to prompt discussion and reflection on a range of school improvement issues. Participative workshop sessions also form part of the programme.

Validated Self-Review

The experience of the schools

It is recognized that a combination of pressure and support can be very powerful in prompting the improvement process, and that the LEA can have an important part to play in challenging schools to achieve enhanced levels of success – and in addition in supporting their efforts to do so. To what extent has the LEA got this pressure and support balance right through the operation of the SIPs initiatives? What were the gains and benefits to schools from participating in these initiatives? In what specific ways have the SIPs been an effective vehicle for the LEA to promote improvement? To answer these questions, the views of a small number of schools were canvassed about their involvement in the SIPs, the contribution that the SIP process had made to the development of quality within the school and the effectiveness of the LEA contribution to this partnership for quality enhancement.

We feel that the case study in Chapter 6 is evidence that validated self-review does work. Of course it is not as administratively tidy as external inspection against a national framework, but we argue that the process of teaching and learning cannot be cabined and confined.

In an article in the *Times Educational Supplement*, Tim Brighouse (1997) drew attention to the unpublished report of the OFSTED visit to Kenmore School in New York State, where they have adopted a model of school improvement which specifies that:

- improvement is a long-term process, involving all schools
- the school is the key unit in development
- improvement is underpinned by a clearly established philosophy
- strategies for improvement are reinforced by regular monitoring of effectiveness and the enhancement of professional skills
- the emphasis is on positive reinforcement to reach goals agreed through consensus, not on external imposition of sanctions

The model depends upon the climate/ethos of schools to foster real improvements in learning, and we believe there is much evidence, as shown in the case study, that there is a third way to improving quality in education – validated self-review.

6 Improving Quality Through a Productive Partnership
A Case Study

> All the evidence indicates that standards rise fastest where schools themselves take responsibility for their own improvement. But schools need the right balance of pressure and support from central and local government.
> (DfEE, 1997a, paragraph 1, p. 24)

The background to this case study is described at the end of Chapter 5: the detailed evidence from the five schools is presented here.

ST ANDREW'S PRIMARY

'A motivating force...pushing the school forward'

St Andrew's is a Church of England Voluntary Aided Primary School with a Nursery. The school intake is almost exclusively from the Bangladeshi community in which it is situated, and all the children in the school speak English as an additional language. Approximately 60 per cent of the children are eligible to receive free school meals. The school participated in the first round of School Improvement Projects (SIPs) which began in 1995/96, and continued this involvement in 1996/97 and 1997/98. These SIPs have been coordinated by the headteacher or deputy headteacher in the school. This senior management lead, and backing, have been important in affirming the significance of the SIPs to the school's development and ensuring time and resources would be made available to promote and aid its success.

The first SIP in which the school took part focused on continuity and progression in teachers' planning. The need to standardize planning across the school was a target in the School Development Plan (SDP), and this SDP target provided the focus of the SIP initiative. The scheme of work in science was used as the vehicle for scrutiny of planning, which concentrated on one curriculum area in the first instance. The SIP process began first of all with the formulation of a SIP action plan for the school. The role of the school's link adviser in collaborating with the school in this process was valuable and useful in the expertise and advice which he brought and the way in which he helped the senior management team (SMT) to 'crystallize our thoughts'. The school welcomed the time and opportunity that the SIPs conferences had allowed the SMT to work on the action plan and to share their action planning process with other schools in the same project. The school's link adviser provided support by attending staff meetings to offer input to the discussions about the curriculum planning format and to share examples of planning formats used in other schools which the staff examined and drew on to inform the development of their own planning model. Through involvement in this project, the school developed and evaluated the science scheme of work, and this became a model for the format of schemes of work in other areas of the curriculum. In the light of these changes to the medium-term planning, the teachers' weekly planning format was revised to make the strategies for differentiation more explicit.

Effective Teaching

The work on planning in the first SIP led the school to progress naturally into a further review project which was seen as an opportunity to consolidate and extend the work already undertaken. Thus the following year the school decided to participate in the Effective Teaching SIP, seeing this as a vehicle for monitoring the effect of the new planning procedures on the quality of teaching and learning in the school. This Effective Teaching Project ran for one year and the school decided to participate again for a further year in this SIP. Teaching and learning in maths was used as the focus for this project and, again, the process began by the formulation of a School Improvement Action Plan being drawn up by SMT and SDS personnel. School staff shared in the construction of the criteria to be used for observing their teaching of maths, and these classroom observations were then carried out by the headteacher, deputy headteacher, a senior teacher and the assessment coordinator. In addition, the deputy headteacher, who also had the role of maths coordinator in the school, examined samples of children's work in maths across all age groups and different abilities and interviewed a number of children about their work in maths. The criteria for monitoring pupils' work were explicit and shared with staff. These included criteria which directly tested the application of work on the previous SIP: for example through checking to see if evidence could be found of continuity and progression in children's learning and evidence of differentiated work.

The views of the LEA maths adviser were canvassed and suggestions for further development in this area of the curriculum were sought from her. The findings from the classroom monitoring observations and the monitoring of pupils' work were analysed and this statistical analysis was presented to the staff, together with a list of the issues raised. While many strengths emerged from this, there were also outcomes which became apparent for the school to address. It was through the vehicle of the SIP initiative that these issues had come to light. Having begun to tackle and work through this agenda, the SMT monitored teaching effectiveness, this time in the teaching of science. This exercise showed a development in teaching quality and evidence that the outcomes from the previous monitoring exercise had influenced classroom practice.

The school valued its participation in the SIP process and cited many benefits from this involvement. Through participation in these initiatives, the school had concentrated its efforts on the improvement process which was driven along by the action plan targets and a specific timescale to which the school had committed itself. When the LEA pressure and support role worked well, the school felt enabled in its efforts to attain its SIP targets and was kept on course to do so within the agreed timescale through the promptings of the LEA advisers and SIP coordinators. When this pressure was not felt so keenly by the school, other imperatives had tended to assume priority and deflect from achievement of the SIP targets. There was a tendency in these circumstances for the school to wander and drift a little from its original plan. The shared view of the headteacher and deputy headteacher was that a combination of both post-OFSTED fatigue following a recent OFSTED inspection, together with rather less pressure and prompting being exerted from the LEA, meant that the action plan deadlines and targets had slipped and some of the impetus from involvement in the first two SIPs had been lost as a result. Where LEA advisers and SIP coordinators had themselves been keen advocates of the SIP process and its benefits, this enthusiasm and energy had been a driving force, motivating the school to pursue its targets. However, given the other pressures on the time and energies of schools, it was felt that it must be a valuable part of the LEA role to prompt the school to maintain the momentum, to stay on course and to continue to make the SIPs work a priority.

A Force for Improvement

Involvement in SIPs had brought clear benefits to a school which was a keen advocate of the SIPs process as a force for improvement. The school had experienced specific gains in terms of short- and medium-term planning leading to more coherence being achieved in planning across the age range; to a better match of work to different abilities; and to an enhanced strategy to achieve progression and continuity in children's skills, knowledge and understanding across the school. This work on planning across the school had involved staff in collaborative cross-phase planning, working across each of the four organizational units which the school employs – Early Years, Key Stage One, Lower Key Stage Two and Upper Key Stage Two – meaning that a teacher who worked in the Early Years unit would perhaps find themselves discussing planning with a member of the Upper Key Stage Two team. This had been a developmental experience for staff, giving teachers a broader picture of planned development across the age range and a wider whole-school view. Teachers with middle management roles in the school had been engaged in leading staff meetings, analysing statistics and other tasks as part of the SIPs process. It was felt that much of this had been a valuable learning experience and one which had prompted the acquisition of some important senior management skills. Improvements had been made in making teaching more effective through the classroom observations and monitoring of children's work. This monitoring process had given the senior management of the school a clearer view of the quality of teaching and learning and alerted them to areas of weakness. The process had also prompted staff to develop as reflective practitioners, more aware of and confident about the strengths of their own practice and also of the issues they needed to embrace.

The SIP initiative was seen by senior management as having acted as a motivating force for improvement and having had clear benefits to the school. The external, impartial viewpoint of an LEA adviser coming into the school was seen as entirely beneficial and was welcomed as a valuable source of expertise, available to the school to draw upon. The school recognized the dangers of just 'ticking along at our own pace', and when this external pressure had worked well it had acted as a driving force, spurring the school on to achieve its targets and deadlines and not losing sight of its goals and purposes.

Network meetings of all the SIP schools in a particular project, facilitated by the SDS, were attended by the school senior management team. While valuable in many ways, they were felt to have limitations, in terms of the difficulty of finding common points of reference between projects when each took a slightly different and specific focus in its own particular context. The SIPs residential and day conferences for project schools, organized by the SDS, were regarded as extremely useful and worthwhile. The high-quality guest speakers had stimulated thought and development, and raised awareness of school improvement issues. The time built into the conference programme for the school's SMT to work on its own action plan was emphasized as something which had been of immense benefit. The difficulties associated with organizing protected and uninterrupted time in school in order to engage in this sort of activity meant that having this quality time to plan and reflect, as part of the conference programme, was essential to the progress of the project in the school. The school was invited to address one of the conferences in order to disseminate its experience of the SIP process to other schools. The headteacher addressed an SIP conference for this purpose, and wrote up a detailed account of the project in the school as a case study which was featured in one of the SIP newsletters circulated to schools.

Evaluation

The school conducted its own formative and summative evaluations of the project to assess the extent to which the action plan targets had been met, and an LEA adviser contributed to the final evaluation as the project neared its conclusion. This LEA perspective was considered by the school to have been both rigorous and a useful source of pressure. When the school considered it had got things just about right, the adviser suggested further improvements which could still be made and the school welcomed the thoroughness, challenge and rigour which was thus injected. The school recognized that there can be a danger of insularity and introspection when reviewing one's own efforts and a danger that a school might indulge in a little 'self congratulatory backslapping'. Participating in the SIP was seen by the school to be a searching experience and one through which it was opened up to both self scrutiny and external examination. The adviser would pose challenging questions and cause the school staff to revisit aspects of their own evaluation in a more critical way, and so improve even further on the advances already made:

> Having looked at the short-term planning, we thought it was pretty good, but the LEA adviser's evaluation was very rigorous and, having thought we'd got it right, he came in and we hadn't got it right...so we had to go back to the staff; it needed a bit of fine tuning. Part of the action plan was to have this external evaluation of what we'd done...so, feeling pretty good about what we'd done, we then got brought back down to earth by the LEA adviser, but that was his rigorous nature. We often think he applies too much rigour...but in terms of differentiation it wasn't fine tuned enough for the lesser and lower ability bands.
>
> (Headteacher)

The headteacher made the point that this sort of rigorous, external viewpoint meant that going into a SIP was definitely not a 'soft option', as the school knew and accepted that the process was going to be a fairly demanding one. Regarding the most valued aspects of LEA support for school improvement, the headteacher put the rigorous external viewpoint, the hard challenging questions and the stimulus to the school's thinking that these things brought, as number one in importance in terms of usefulness in moving the school on.

The LEA advisers and project coordinators had brought a rigour to the school's own monitoring and evaluation of progress. The challenge posed to the school's thinking was seen as entirely beneficial in moving the school forward. The expertise of LEA personnel was regarded by the school as having made a direct contribution to the school improvement process, especially the initial collaboration and support given to the process of constructing the SIP action plan.

Reflecting on the school's involvement in SIPs for three years, the headteacher commented:

> Over the three years it has been a motivating force and I think it has had the additional external viewpoint of OFSTED because it was commented on favourably that we'd done a lot of good work and they [the OFSTED inspectors] were especially keen on the way the middle managers' role had been developed and I think that was very much linked up with SIPs.

The deputy headteacher also felt that involvement in SIPs had been a spur to improvement, keeping the school focused on the planned process of school development:

> It was a really good vehicle for us. What we've felt through this is that it has given us a plan and a timescale to do it in, so we've been a lot more 'on task' through being in the project than if we'd just done it ourselves. It was extremely useful and it was a very good tool for pushing the school forward.

The headteacher affirmed that the SIPs process had been 'definitely beneficial' having considerable gains for the curriculum planning procedures and schemes of work, for implementation of differentiation strategies and for monitoring teaching and learning which had given the SMT a clearer view of quality across the school. The deputy headteacher shared this view, saying: 'There have been improvements in the teaching, and in what is being taught and how it is taught as well'.

Other indirect benefits to result from the SIPs process, such as development of skills and confidence for middle managers and enhanced collaborative cross-phase planning, were also valued. The school had entered the SIPs process in the expectation that it would mobilize the school and act as a catalyst for improvement. This had indeed proved to be the case. The headteacher reflected on the hopes the school had for the SIP when they first took the decision to participate:

> It would provide expertise and it would timetable it and provide deadlines that you perhaps wouldn't normally meet with other things coming along, but knowing that you've got an action plan with deadlines we felt it was going to drive us along.

The deputy headteacher also made this point about the value of having access to the expertise of the LEA advisory team: 'It's their expertise as well...we tend only to see what's going on here...they can share with us suggestions of things that might work and suggestions of things that we hadn't thought of.'

TEESDALE PRIMARY

> 'Continually refining and reviewing our practice'

This school is a county primary school with a nursery. The housing in its catchment area is, in the main, terraced properties and council-owned properties, and about a quarter of the pupils at the school are entitled to free school meals. For approximately one-fifth of the school population, the first language of the home is a language other than English. The school has maintained a continued involvement in SIPs for three consecutive years, beginning with the launch of the first projects in 1995/96. Why did the school first decide to participate in the SIP initiative?

> Obviously you like to think the school is about school improvement and continually refining and reviewing our practice and so it seemed to give us a vehicle for that.
>
> (Headteacher)

The pace of change for schools can be frenzied and it was felt that the deadlines imposed by the SIP action plan would be a useful discipline and focus to keep planned developments on track:

> It is a positive thing to be given a deadline. In the hectic life of schools I think to have somebody externally saying 'Have you done that?' – not in a threatening way – I think that was useful.
>
> (Deputy headteacher)

There were some initial concerns about taking on something else in addition to the many development targets to which the school had already committed itself, but it soon became apparent that the SIPs work was not an 'add-on' but a means by which to pursue many of the school's identified development priorities:

> I felt at first, 'Oh no, its something else we've got to do, it's sort of on top of everything else'. I thought, 'So right, I've got to get my head round this.' But actually as it's gone on and quite soon after we got involved, I began to see that it was part of the Development Plan – it was actually what we might be doing anyway – but it was just a method of carrying it through really...so it's integrated into what we're doing

rather than you're doing all your work then you've got to do this extra bit.

(Deputy headteacher)

Reviewing Curriculum Planning

The school was committed to moving forward and had its own clear route mapped out in terms of future development. The SIP was used as the mechanism through which development targets would be pursued, and it would bring with it access to school improvement conferences and a range of other LEA support to feed into and stimulate development activity. The focus of the first SIP in 1995/96 was a review of planning procedures as part of the Continuity and Progression School Improvement Project. The school had identified, as one of its development targets, the need to simplify the schemes of work and to have a system in place to map children's acquisition of skills and knowledge in order to avoid gaps and repetition. So it was decided that this would be incorporated into the first SIP, focusing on the subject area of English. Through the SIP the school reviewed its long-, medium- and short-term curriculum planning and the staff worked together to devise a new matrix planning format to be trailled in planning English. The school received support from its link adviser, who helped the school to formulate its SIP action plan, and the expertise of another LEA adviser was drawn upon to assist the staff in their review of planning procedures. The school had an OFSTED inspection in March 1996, and many of the key issues for development resulting from this inspection were followed up as part of the SIP. Schemes of work and the development of writing across the curriculum were two of the OFSTED key issues and, as post-OFSTED action plan targets, these became the focus for school improvement work. Post-OFSTED action planning funding was used to buy into the School Improvement Project in 1996/97 for this purpose. In 1996/97 the focus on writing was an important part of the SIP and the school again had effective support from the LEA in this task through an LEA adviser working with the staff on the development of writing. The review of planning was extended to include another of the core subjects; this time it was the turn of planning in maths to come under scrutiny, with input from one of the LEA SIP coordinators at a residential weekend arranged so that staff could work on planning in maths. This was considered to have been helpful in guiding the work, but this improvement work was not to the exclusion of the school's own identified development targets, for it also pursued the development of information and computer technology and music as part of the SIP. In 1997/98 the development of the two curriculum areas of history and art became the focus of the SIP, having been identified as targets in the SDP. Schemes of work in history were revised to improve planning for continuity and progression, and the focus for art was for teachers and support staff to practise their skills and also to acquire new skills and techniques.

In these ways, the SIP work became a vehicle for furthering the school development plan priorities and the key issues in the post-OFSTED action plan:

> The OFSTED inspection drove some of the targets that were set, looking at the schemes of work particularly, because that was something that had been identified....The OFSTED inspectors were happy with the quality of teaching and learning but it was looking at the structure and more long-term planning and I think that then fed into it.
>
> (Deputy headteacher)

Refining the School's Thinking

Not only was the school's LEA SIP coordinator's input on the construction of the SIP action plan useful, but talking through the action plan at one of the SIP group meetings with LEA SIP personnel also helped to refine the school's thinking and to suggest, in a supportive way, possible revisions which might enhance the plan further. The school has established the practice of conducting a review of the school development plan at the end of each academic year and, as targets from the SDP had transferred into the SIP action plan, this review incorporated an examination of progress made towards the SIP action plan targets. The staff and governors are involved in this annual review, which is also attended by the school's link adviser.

The network meetings for participating schools were felt to have been a less useful aspect of involvement in the projects. It was felt that these meetings were rather too general in nature and so failed to address the particular needs and concerns of individual schools. At network meetings, those schools with projects which were well under way and past the initial planning stages felt that the network meetings had little to offer and few benefits could be gained from them. Network meetings in general were not considered to be a particular benefit from the project involvement, largely due to the individual nature of the projects and their very specific focuses which could constrain the ability to share across projects and transfer experience from one individual school context to another.

A Valuable Opportunity for Dissemination and Sharing

As part of the SIPs, the LEA organizes residential and day conferences for participating schools. The school was asked by the LEA to make a presentation to other schools at one of these conferences about the development and impact of the SIP in the school. This dissemination was in itself a very valuable part of the SIP process as it made the school reflect on its SIP involvement and ponder on the experience and the gains for the school:

> I felt those presentations, more than anything else, crystallized what we'd been doing, and it helped because you've got to stand up and you've got to present your project; therefore you've got to have your ideas clear. You've got to look back and review and evaluate what you've done. So I think for this school that was particularly useful.
>
> (Deputy headteacher)

The Senior Management Team also felt the conferences to have been a very beneficial aspect of involvement in the SIP programme because of the quality of the keynote speakers, the workshops and the protected time it afforded the headteacher and the SIP coordinator to work together on the action plan. The keynote speakers provided inspiration and motivation, which brought back and injected renewed vigour to share with colleagues at school. Participation in the conferences and the opportunities these brought to share with others provided affirmation to the school that they were 'on the right track' and reinforced the value of the work they were doing. The headteacher reflected that:

> We liked the keynote speakers, we liked some of the workshops where you get a chance to discuss some of the issues...but we did take some time out where we worked on something for the school improvement that we wanted to do on our own and we valued the time.

The school benefited from an injection of LEA expertise when it organized its own school residential conference for teaching and non-teaching staff as part of the SIP target to develop art. The conference was an opportunity for staff to enhance and extend their art skills and techniques and, as part of the SIP package of support, a number of workshops were provided for staff and these were facilitated by LEA personnel. The deputy headteacher reported that the school had received a lot of input from the LEA through the SIP.

Evaluation

The school is firmly of the view that its involvement in the SIP has been a beneficial experience in terms of promoting its on-going development. The conferences have been of value in keeping the school up to date with school improvement research and thinking, in providing opportunities to share with others and in affording occasions to listen to speakers who were themselves sources of inspiration which stimulated fresh thinking. The conferences also provided protected time, allowing the headteacher and the SIP coordinator to work closely together on development issues without interruptions and distractions, and this protected time was highly valued and well used.

One important benefit identified by the school from its SIPs involvement was that of giving focus and immediacy to its on-going school improvement work and extending opportunities for collegiate ways of working. The SIP, it was felt, had focused school development work, staff meetings and staff training activities a lot more. These two points were summed up by the deputy headteacher, who said:

> I think it is the focus that it provides and the external checks, not in a heavy way, but it helps to keep you moving....The long term benefit for staff, I feel, is this feeling of developing together, the ownership issue, working together.

The headteacher saw the SIP involvement as not only sharpening the focus of development activity but also remarked that:

> It has given us different ways of looking at how we do develop. We put most of this development activity under the SIP umbrella.

The headteacher has close links with the LEA, was active in many new developments with working groups and was, for a period of time, seconded to work for the authority on support for newly qualified teachers. She therefore had close ties with the SDS, was aware of current developments and thinking across a broader front and saw the SIP as part of the whole pattern of her own and the school's wider involvement with the authority. This involvement embraced her own attendance at primary conferences for headteachers which the authority organizes and which also have keynote speakers of national repute; the attendance of staff from the school at in-service training sessions; ten- and twenty-day training courses for subject specialists which the LEA operates, funded by the DfEE Grant for Education Support and Training (GEST); training for school governors; pre- and post-OFSTED support; and support for school self-review through the school's liaison adviser and education development officers. All of these things are recognized as contributing to school improvement, and they represent a range of support to which the school has ready access as a subscriber to one of the service-level agreement packages with the LEA. The SIP initiatives are seen by the school as yet one further aspect of the many ways in which the LEA supports the school's development. As an experienced headteacher of ten years standing, she has a confident approach to change and development. She feels that it is the responsibility of the school to take the initiative to seek expertise and assistance from the LEA as these are appropriate to the needs of the school, and that this is part of the spirit and ethos of self-determination and autonomy which characterize the way in which schools now operate. The headteacher feels that the school has its own internally generated drive for improvement and that this is embedded within its culture. Setting and defining this improvement culture, she feels, has been a strong and important feature of the LEA role.

> I think a lot of that culture did come through the LEA. I give the LEA a lot of credit for that culture that was developed in me and that I hope I've developed here. I think it's the culture of the authority.

The SIPs therefore have to be seen as part of the LEA culture of school improvement and the impact of this must not be overlooked.

The school's involvement in the SIP initiatives is seen by the senior management team as an experience which has been valuable in reaffirming the school's internally generated drive for improvement; challenging the school with new ideas and new thinking; and assisting the improvement process through the targeted involvement of LEA personnel.

In the experiences of Teesdale primary we see the role of the LEA clearly defined as that of 'critical friend' and the integral nature of the SIP as helping to meet the school's own development programme in more considered ways.

CHADWICK INFANTS

> 'Not an event but a journey'

Chadwick Infants is a county infant school with a nursery. It is situated in an area of the borough which is characterized by high levels of disadvantage and unemployment. About 40 per cent of the children are entitled to free school meals. All the children have English as an additional language. The school entered the SIP initiative as part of the second wave of projects launched in 1996/97. The headteacher and deputy headteacher attended a conference organized by the LEA at which a number of schools that had taken part in the first round of SIPs in 1995/6 were invited to make presentations to share this experience with other schools considering participation in 1996/97 as a possibility. Any initial concerns held by the school's SMT that the projects would be controlled by the LEA rather than schools themselves were dispelled at this conference as the respective roles and responsibilities of the LEA and schools were defined and it became clear that the ownership of the projects and responsibility for them lay firmly within the domain of the schools themselves. The school's liaison adviser furnished the school with more information about the projects, and the staff were consulted by SMT members at smaller meetings of teams of staff before meeting together as a whole staff to reach final agreement. There were some initial worries and concerns among staff that there might be a lot of extra work involved, but these fears were eased when it became apparent that the project was a means of taking forward an identified development priority and as such would not be an 'add-on' but integral to the pursuit of agreed aims and targets. Chadwick's Language Coordinator said:

> I would say, I think, that because we are very much conscious of being a school where all our children are second language learners, we felt that anything that was going to further develop the language within school was going to be of benefit.

Thus an agreement was reached that the school would take part as it was felt that this would be a beneficial means of pursuing an identified need, and the deputy headteacher became the SIP coordinator in this first year of involvement. The school had already identified the need to improve children's reading as a target for future development and it was felt that participation in the Improving Literacy SIP would be of benefit as a means to achieve this aim.

English Language Development for Multi-lingual Learners

The school was very conscious of the need to improve English language development, as all the children at the school have English as an additional language. This was a priority as a development area, and the headteacher and deputy headteacher had already carried out some data collection which revealed that one of the three reception classes was not achieving to the same standard as the others, and this was a cause for concern. It was also decided that it was important to begin with the Reception Year in order to lay a firm foundation for good language work to be developed across the school. It was agreed, though, that the SIP focus would not be restricted to one year group but instead that this would form part of a wider focus on exciting and creative ways of teaching literacy across the school. It was hoped that among the benefits would be an extension to the range of strategies used by staff in developing children's language competencies and also support for new staff in developing their skills to meet the range of needs of children at different stages as learners of English as an additional language. The Language Coordinator was centrally involved in the decision to take language development as the focus of the SIP and work got underway in the reception classes.

One important development on which the school focused was planning and developing pre-reading and reading activities which would encourage differentiated language work. Core vocabulary relating to the reading scheme was examined and differentiated activities planned to meet the range of language needs. The outcome was the production of a pack of differentiated activities to meet a range of needs and abilities, and this is used by the teachers of the reception classes in planning the reading activities for the year. Also, as part of this project, portfolios of children's work were compiled, and these have proved a useful support for the newly qualified teacher in particular, who has been able to see the standard which children are expected to achieve. This has been a ready yardstick for the teacher, without the benefit of many years experience, to refer to when assessing the standard achieved by her class in relation to that expected for children of that age.

> Our newly qualified teacher found it useful because she can look at the activity, go and get the portfolio, and look at the work that the children have done and she knows what she's aiming for.
>
> (Deputy headteacher)

Clear gains were demonstrated from data collected by the school Senior Management Team. This quantitative data was used to inform the evaluation of the success of the SIP developments in the school in terms of raising standards. In the Reception Year, all the children were worked with, with data collected for ten children from each class for monitoring purposes. A range of their assessments was considered in July 1996 and again in July 1997. This involved their Needs Assessment Scores, which are used for special funding under Section 11 of the Local Government Act (1966). In addition, scores from the Local Education Authority's own Baseline Assessment, and the key word acquisition scores recorded on the school's own internal pupil records, were used. This exercise produced quantifiable data showing clear evidence of the added value gained from involvement in the SIP in terms of the improved progress being made by the children, who demonstrated distinct advancement in the acquisition of key words. This sample of pupils has been tracked in subsequent years so that the pace of their progress can continue to be monitored.

Another part of the SIPs initiative in the school was to develop a closer working partnership with parents in promoting children's language development. The school held a meeting with parents to discuss with them the different ways in which they could support reading at home, and this meeting was a great success in terms of the number of parents attending and the interest they showed in becoming more involved. An LEA adviser attended this meeting to address the parents and explain to them the aims of the project and what the school was trying to achieve. Following this meeting a few parents visited the classes during the school day to experience language teaching taking place, thus gaining a better understanding and becoming more confident themselves as co-educators. The school begins the day each morning with parents being welcomed into the classes when they accompany their children to school and being encouraged to stay and engage in the range of activities taking place in the classrooms, and these include language-based activities. A home activity pack was developed, which included verbal tasks which the school first explained to the parents and

Improving Quality Through a Productive Partnership

which the parents were then encouraged to try at home with their children. This activity pack was developed to meet the particular needs of the families whom the school serves, taking into account the linguistic background of the home. The school thus worked with parents on home reading activities and literacy-based tasks which parents might wish to share with their children at home. The school had received some funding from the Single Regeneration Budget to support family literacy and this complemented the work being undertaken as part of the SIP initiative.

As part of the wider school focus on language development the language coordinator organized a very successful 'book week' at the school, and this took place towards the end of the first year of the school's SIP involvement. Events during this week included visits to the school from authors, illustrators, the Literature Development Officer from the local library and a display of books from a local bookstore. Among the language development activities offered to the children were: bilingual storytelling; poetry writing; a puppet show for nursery and reception children; a visit from junior-aged children from another school to help with reading activities; and children making their own books, ranging from simple paper folding to books in boxes. The week served to heighten the focus on language, to stimulate interest and parental involvement and to further the wider purposes of the SIP.

LEA Support and Involvement

The school benefited from the support of its link adviser in the initial stages of drawing up the SIP action plan. SDS personnel also attended staff meetings to offer advice and ideas and helped the school to arrange outside speakers to contribute to staff development work related to the targets of the SIP action plan. At the request of the school, an LEA adviser also carried out a resource audit of stocks of fiction and non-fiction books, and this included a questionnaire to staff about the book provision in each school area. The information from the audit was collated and analysed and this led to the creation of two new library areas in the school and the purchase of additional books.

The day and residential SIPs conferences were valued by the school. These events provided the opportunity to listen to speakers of national standing; and the time built into the programme for school delegates to work together on planning, without the interruptions which can hinder progress on this work in school, was considered particularly valuable. The conferences were also seen as providing encouragement which stimulated further development and helped to guard against too much introspection: 'It gives you that spurt to continue, a buzz of enthusiasm.' The deputy headteacher had been invited to make presentations at SIP conferences in order to disseminate project outcomes to a wider audience and share some of the expertise which the school had gained through its involvement in the project:

> We did a presentation of the stage we had reached and that was interesting because schools were very open in explaining where they were up to and asking us about different things that we'd tried that had been successful.
>
> (Headteacher)

The SIP network meetings were considered to have some benefits in the opportunities they afforded for discussion and sharing ideas, but were also rather too general to address individual issues related to a specific context. The SIPs newsletters circulated to schools by the LEA and sometimes containing updates from participating schools on developments and progress were considered useful. Commenting on the range of LEA support which the school had experienced, the deputy headteacher said that 'LEA personnel come in to assist with the writing of the action plan they support you along…the conferences that they offer are very, very good'.

Evaluation

Real and demonstrable gains resulted from involvement in the SIP initiative. These included:

- the development of expertise in quantitative data collection and analysis
- the development of a differentiated activity pack which has served as an important resource for language work
- the generation of portfolios of children's work which have provided a useful guide for newly qualified teachers in assessing standards
- the development of activities for supporting parents and children on home reading and helping parents to become more involved as co-educators in partnership with teachers
- an audit of the range of books available in the school, leading to an increase in the breadth and variety of reading material available to children
- a review of children's reading records
- the development of more comprehensive school policies for handwriting and speaking and listening

Through the collection of quantitative data it was possible to demonstrate evidence of progress in language development, and improvements were made in measuring and recording progress in reading. The headteacher commented that the results had been very satisfying and that the teachers could see marked improvements. The teachers themselves had been committed to the project, seeing it as worthwhile:

> The staff have been very supportive of the whole project, they've really been involved...It's raised issues along the way that the whole staff have taken on board and we've discussed.
>
> (Headteacher)

The deputy headteacher confirmed the gains to the school from involvement in the project which she described as having been 'very beneficial...very, very worthwhile'.

The termly visit of the school's link adviser included monitoring of progress with the SIP and, towards the end of the year, support for evaluation of what had been accomplished in terms of meeting the action plan targets. The action plan played an important part in helping to promote the pace of development and to discourage 'drifting' from the agreed priorities. In these ways the action plan was seen to have imposed a discipline, and without this the school felt that the progress made would not have been so great. The action plan imposed pressures of time on the school which helped to drive the pace of progress. However, an OFSTED school inspection during the second year of the project meant that the rate of progress had been slower than the school would have wished, as efforts had switched to preparation for the inspection.

Throughout the project it was felt that the LEA had been a motivating force, helping to keep the spotlight on the SIP when there were dangers of becoming distracted by other demands and pressures which are part of school life. The deputy headteacher made this point, saying that:

> sometimes when you start things off, other things take over, but you know with this you've got guidelines behind you. Because the LEA is there behind you, guiding you, and conferences come along that you go to, it keeps you constantly reminded of what you are focusing on. I think that is a big plus from the LEA. You are also aware that someone is going to come in at the end of the year and look at and evaluate your action plan.

The LEA was recognized as a source of support which was always there and available for the school to call upon at any time:

> It's good because we feel that there is support out there. If there was anything that we needed or we wanted to find out or we had a problem, we could pick up the phone and somebody would be there to advise.
>
> (Headteacher)

It was felt that the link adviser could act sometimes as a springboard for sounding out new ideas, someone, as the language coordinator remarked, with whom the staff could 'spin off ideas and thoughts'. However, the language coordinator also felt that at times the support available was a little stretched, as each link adviser was attached to many schools and had other duties to fulfil and this means that on occasion the level of support available to an individual school may be 'diluted'. It was also felt that not all LEA personnel involved with the school had a full awareness of the specific issues arising from the particular context of the school, especially the challenges which arise when engaging parents who are non-English speakers themselves in active partnership with the school. Thus it was felt that, on occasion, LEA input to the school had not always had appropriate regard for these sorts of issues.

The impetus and drive for improvement was internally generated within the school by the shared ambition among the staff to raise standards and to increase effectiveness. The headteacher likened this quest to a journey which one is constantly making, rather than a one-off event, and the school intends to continue that journey and its involvement in the SIP initiatives as a way of pursuing the path to school improvement in future years.

WIDEACRE PRIMARY

> 'Proving improvement: translating successful school development into effective school improvement'

Wideacre is a county primary school with a nursery, situated in an urban location within the borough. Approximately 35 per cent of the children are entitled to free school meals and over half of the children are claimants of the clothing grant allowance. One-third of the children are of Asian heritage and have English as an additional language. On taking up his post at the school, the headteacher realized that the school needed to refocus attention on the processes of teaching and learning, the core business of every school. This had also been highlighted as a priority for future school development in the school's OFSTED report and there was widespread recognition among the staff, too, that standards of achievement needed to improve. At the end of both Key Stages One and Two, the school's National Curriculum assessment results in all the core subjects were below both LEA averages and national averages in terms of the expected levels of achievement for children at ages 7 and 11.

However, there was a determination among the staff to effect improvements and a shared view that, while the school might be above average in terms of indicators of disadvantage and that there might be little the school could do to impact on that, nevertheless something could be done about levels of attainment. With this background of poor standards of achievement, a new and committed headteacher with a vision for change and a keen desire on the part of the staff to effect improvements, the school was ready to move forward.

The headteacher recognized that having a very professional and confident team of staff to work with was a huge bonus in terms of initiating a change process, as a state of readiness existed to embrace change and to effect improvements. In a school above national and LEA averages in terms of indicators of social disadvantage, a less professional and committed body of staff might have used this as an excuse for complacency by assuming low expectations. However, in Wideacre Primary school quite the reverse was true, the staff being determined to provide learning opportunities of the highest possible quality and to promote high standards of achievement. The headteacher's vision had helped to establish an achievement culture in the school with high expectations of all children, regardless of socio-economic background:

> We had high expectations, we had a vision for the school, we were clear of what the school was about....There was a high degree of acceptance from the staff that socio-economic deprivation was not going to prevent us from having high levels of achievement...that says something about the quality of the staff.

The school framed four searching key questions as the starting point for self-scrutiny:

- How well do we think are we doing?
- How well are we actually doing compared with other schools in similar circumstances?
- What more should we do to achieve?
- What must we do to make it happen?

School Improvement

> 'We were about school improvement in everything we did'

The school engaged with the SIPs in 1996/97 and signed up for the project on 'Raising achievement through effective curriculum management'. Rather than seeing this as a project in its own right and, as such, separate from, or an 'add-on' to, the on-going process of school development, the school felt it important to integrate the SIP into the process of whole-school development and change. The school took time to reflect on what role a school improvement project might play in the agenda for change which it had set itself:

> We didn't sign up at first because I couldn't see where this would fit in...we had a School Development Plan that was comprehensive and it

> included a process for school improvement in a sense, and we were about school improvement in everything we did, so why did we want to do another project? We had a post-OFSTED action plan and a School Development Plan – why did we want to have this 'add-on' which didn't seem to fit in with anything else?
>
> (Headteacher)

There were some philosophical misgivings about a school improvement 'project' existing as a discrete entity, with its own action plan and targets, when teaching, learning, pupil progress and the curriculum were recognized to be central to the core purpose of the school and, as such, at the centre of all its development processes. The term 'project' in this sense is perhaps something of a misnomer inasmuch as it implies an initiative existing in its own right with a beginning and an end. In fact, the school recognized that what was needed was not a 'project' to be added-on to its development agenda but an improvement process to become embedded into all aspects of development.

> This was the philosophy...by doing that project you will actually learn about a process and eventually you will drop the 'project' bit and you will adopt a school improvement process.
>
> (Headteacher)

While still having these reservations about the nature of a 'project' for improvement and its place in the process of development, the school joined the SIP, seeing it particularly as a means of sharing in the collegiate aspects of networking and the other benefits which formal membership of a project would bring.

One of the first tasks was to formulate a SIP action plan, and here the LEA provided valuable assistance, particularly in offering advice and guidance to the headteacher on action planning techniques and so helping to improve the effectiveness of school action planning:

> That was where the first part of the LEA positive involvement came in because they certainly helped me refine my action planning technique very much. I learnt a lot about more effective action planning.
>
> (Headteacher)

The LEA also provided the school with school performance data which was an excellent source of information with which the school could appraise its own strengths and weaknesses and also use as a basis for comparison of its own standards against those attained by other similar schools. The school realized that if it was to pursue improvement in considered and informed ways then this sort of data was essential in helping to review itself and establish a baseline from which to measure improvements in success:

> Data is important from the LEA – excellent school performance data and comparative data – that's really important. If you're serious about school improvement then you need hard data to show what's effective and what isn't, so that was really crucial, I felt.
>
> (Headteacher)

The project became part of the process of school development and, while an SIP action plan had been written at the start of the project, the school experienced some difficulty in working to this as something separate from the SDP, the priorities for the SDP being centrally focused on pupil progress and achievement. The objectives of the SIP action plan then became subsumed within the school development plan and therefore were pursued through the development plan priorities rather than as a separate change programme. The school development plan adopted a nomenclature which identified, for each agreed priority: the actions needed; the person(s) responsible; the monitoring arrangements; time needed; resource and financial implications; and success criteria. The SIP was prioritized and described in this way, which was thus consistent with, and integrated into, the school's own way of development planning.

Gaining Commitment

At Wideacre the headteacher took a very proactive stance in leading whole-school development but was aware of the need to gain the commitment of stakeholders. He did this by consulting teachers, parents and governors to establish an understanding of their perceptions of the school's strengths and weaknesses, and then by using this data to inform the process of establishing development priorities. All the data collected was analysed and the results reported back to the school staff and governors, and a small working group was established to draw up the school development plan. The overall focus of the SDP was to raise achievement, and one target in pursuit of this was to re-examine the role of curriculum coordinators in managing quality and standards across the school in each of the curriculum areas for which they had responsibility.

It was decided that, in order for curriculum coordinators to form a view of quality and standards, they would need release from teaching so that they could visit classrooms and monitor the extent to which school policy was being carried out in practice. Thus time was costed into the SDP to enable this to happen, and this monitoring process took place across all subjects of the curriculum with members of the governors' curriculum committee also being involved. Curriculum coordinators were given half a day per week over a term to visit classrooms and monitor the quality of teaching and learning in their subjects. This had a beneficial impact on practice and allowed coordinators the opportunity to gain a view of quality and standards across the age range. The headteacher believed that, more than anything else, this strategy had a profound effect on teaching throughout the school. Each subject coordinator was given the half-day per week in the term following the formulation of the subject policy statement, so that the coordinator could see how the subject policy was impacting on classroom practice. The coordinators used this time as an opportunity to teach the classes alongside the class teachers, and in the following term the coordinator would revisit classes to monitor and assess progress in developing that area of the curriculum. Each curriculum area in turn followed this cycle of initial visits and follow-up visits to classes in order to work alongside colleagues and to monitor standards and quality.

Following this, the curriculum coordinators and governors held an evening meeting at which each curriculum coordinator was allocated five minutes to report on their subject area and what they had identified as priorities for its future development across the school. In a spirit of partnership and reciprocity, two of the governors presented their impressions to the staff of those aspects of school life which were their particular areas of interest, namely parental involvement and community links.

Evaluation

The school had written its own policy document, entitled 'Proving Improvement: translating successful school development into effective school improvement', which saw the process of whole-school development as the vehicle for school improvement. This policy was grounded in a commitment to self-improvement and was part of the school development planning process. A five-year plan had been carefully constructed, taking into account both the school's own identified priorities and local and national priorities. The philosophy of the headteacher was that the SIP would be one part of this drive towards improvement and what mattered most was that, through the project, a process of improvement would be effected which would itself, in time, become embedded into the development culture of the school. It was not the project as such that was to be of lasting benefit, but the improvement process which it would generate and which, it was hoped, would take root and have lasting effect. The headteacher wondered if this was in fact the longer-term intention of the LEA in instituting the projects: that they would be the vehicle by which a process of improvement within participating schools would become established. He speculated that perhaps this was part of the LEA vision for school improvement, for an improvement process to become embedded within the culture of schools.

Improving Quality Through a Productive Partnership

The school identified many benefits gained from membership of the SIP and these included: the advice and support of the school's link adviser; collaboration with other colleagues at network meetings and SIPs conferences; and the exposure to speakers of national and international reputation at the SIPs conferences, allowing access to current research and thinking in the field of school improvement. The conferences in particular made an impact on how the school perceived itself and the tasks of school improvement:

> Access to national and international speakers and current thinking on school improvement, which not only is it good because the content's good but it actually makes you feel good about what you're doing because you think, hang on a minute, here am I at this little school...and there's people with international reputations coming to talk to us about improvement, and you feel part of something much bigger and also it raises the status of what you're doing.
>
> (Headteacher)

In common with other schools, the time afforded to the school delegates at the conference to reflect, discuss and plan together was considered a great bonus. This uninterrupted time was well used to plan the development tasks and much was achieved in this way. The informal networking with other school delegates which took place at these SIPs conferences was considered in many ways to be of more value than the formal networking meetings arranged by the LEA, and much was gained from discussions and sharing of experience with colleagues outside the planned programme. Of benefit also were the opportunities for schools to disseminate their SIP to other schools through formal presentations to the conference gatherings. This occasion to share in what other schools had been doing, and to learn from their successes and the challenges they had faced in tackling their own agendas for improvement, was considered to offer a valuable opportunity for learning.

One incidental outcome which resulted from the review of the arrangements for curriculum management in the school was the more active involvement of the school governors in school management issues and a closer dialogue between staff and governors on the curriculum:

> We became increasingly aware of the importance of involving governors and that helped to develop our working with governors and to draw them in on a strategic level.
>
> (Headteacher)

The school began to try ways of working with governors that were less a case of 'them and us' and more in the spirit of partners working together in pursuit of a shared task.

Wideacre was led by a headteacher with a vision and a strategy to move the school towards the realization of that vision. He used the results of his stakeholder survey to inform that vision and the construction of development targets. The SIP was one of the strategies used to realize one of the overarching aims – to raise achievement through more effective management of the curriculum. The specific purpose in going into the SIP was to develop a process to effect improvement, rather than to participate in a project. Ultimately, the headteacher saw that the project itself would become obsolete as staff became better informed about, and more proficient with, school improvement as a process, which would have an important role in defining the culture of the school:

> In the end, there never was a project – it became everything – from the word go it was everything. I had this philosophical problem from the beginning with the word 'project' – this is why I found it really difficult to actually tell people what our project was because it never was a single project. We, from the word go, realized it was a process and therefore in a sense we subverted the LEA's School Improvement Project for our own use and purposes which was to get access to those things I've talked about. But we never did a really specific project – we were working on too many fronts – we couldn't isolate anything and say the project did this – it didn't – it did everything.
>
> (Headteacher)

The headteacher felt that it was possibly because the school was already quite well along the road of establishing a culture focused on improvement that there was little intervention on behalf of the LEA. The success enjoyed by the school in tackling the improvement agenda was recognized by the LEA and, while the support which the school received from the LEA brought real benefits, it was felt that a little more challenge and pressure would have spurred the school on to achieve even more. The support received from the LEA confirmed the direction being taken and the progress made, but it was felt by the headteacher that, with rather more challenge, the gains made might have been greater:

> It's policy now, isn't it, that Local Education Authorities intervene in inverse proportion to success, and the LEA was forward thinking enough to be doing that. So, basically we didn't get a lot of support....Support was there when we needed it but, if I'm being perfectly honest, I would have liked some more pressure because we could have done more, I think. I would have liked somebody to challenge – we didn't get the challenge – because it could have been better, we could have done more.
>
> (Headteacher)

The headteacher also recognized that it's not always easy getting the right balance between pressure and support, and that attaining the most effective combination of the two in relation to each school could be a challenge in itself for the LEA.

The school appreciated the recognition by the LEA of the efforts made, and this recognition had a positive impact on staff morale and self esteem – which in itself was a motivation to continue with the improvement tasks. Yet essentially, at its core, the drive for success had its own internal momentum generated by a highly professional, committed and competent staff determined to move forward.

RISING DALE SECONDARY SCHOOL

'Quality through partnership'

Rising Dale is a coeducational comprehensive secondary school taking pupils aged 11 to 16. It is situated between a major city and a large town. There are currently approximately 1,550 students on the roll and approximately ninety teaching staff. The school occupies two sites about 500 metres apart and divided by a minor road. Years 7 and 8 are based at the Lower School site, with Years 9, 10 and 11 at the Upper School site. The proportion of pupils eligible for free school meals is 23 per cent and the proportion of pupils speaking English as an additional language is 3 per cent. The proportion of pupils with special educational needs, including those with 'statements', is 11 per cent. Throughout the five years of compulsory schooling, all pupils experience a common curriculum and all are involved in external examinations in Year 11. The school participated in two School Improvement Projects, and each is described.

Project 1: Monitoring Individual Pupil Progress to Raise Achievement (MIPPRA)

Concern about declines in levels of achievement was the prime motivation prompting the school to participate in the School Improvement Project concerned with monitoring individual pupil progress to raise achievement (MIPPRA). The SIP was known to the LEA by the acronym MIPP, and it is significant to this school that 'RA' was added, thus becoming MIPPRA, because the school was attracted to the project as a means of raising levels of achievement which was a pressing concern.

In 1995 the proportion of pupils achieving 5 or more A–C grades in the General Certificate of Secondary Education (GCSE) was 19 per cent; the following year this figure had declined to 16 per cent:

> The school is bottom heavy in terms of ability. There is no doubt about that. It's not a normal distribution curve in terms of ability, it is bottom heavy, but evidence and research and indicators suggested that we should be above that. So, that was the motivation to become involved – purely and simply to adopt any measures to raise achievement.
>
> (Deputy headteacher)

Senior management and staff at the school also had concerns about a culture of underachievement among certain groups of pupils, and there was a realization that this too must be addressed as part of any strategy aimed at raising achievement. The response was therefore to employ a number of measures aimed at creating a clear focus within the school on achievement. Behind the figures lay a major problem for the school in terms of underachievement in science. Many pupils were not performing well in this subject area, and the problem was compounded because science was a dual award certification subject at GCSE in which only about 6 per cent of pupils were actually achieving grades A–C. There was also the problem of ethos and culture among underachieving pupils which compounded the difficulties, and this needed to be considered.

> My own view of MIPPRA was that if we could put the responsibility on individuals – the 'I' in the acronym – to be responsible for their own achievement, while at the same time we dealt with the longer-term issues of difficulties in the teaching and management of science, then, over the short term, children might be better focused and might – even if they don't improve their science results – try and find that extra grade from somewhere else....And there's absolutely no doubt in my mind that they did manage to do that. I do believe it's a sort of 'back door approach' to raising standards – that you put the onus on children, on target setting, on mentoring....I know it's all fashionable and the buzz words now, but it does seem to have an effect.
>
> (Deputy headteacher)

A core team of staff volunteers was formed to plan and coordinate the strategy, and to monitor progress and outcomes. A detailed MIPPRA action plan was formulated and this lent direction and purpose to the project development. The strategy consisted of a number of initiatives, which included mentoring, academic reviews and more frequent pupil progress reports being sent home. Additionally a variety of assessment data was used to support and inform the process of raising achievement, targets were set, and a closer dialogue with parents was attempted. All this had to run alongside strategies to solve the science problem if the school was to become a higher achieving school.

The detailed MIPPRA action plan described how the school would monitor individual pupil progress to raise achievement, and the strategy was very clear. Integral to the strategy was an enhanced role for parents in this task of raising individual achievement. Consequently, reporting to parents was increased, with progress reports to be sent home each half term, totalling six reports per pupil per year. Target setting was a central strand, and this involved all children and staff in the school. Periodic, formal, structured academic reviews were at the heart of the strategy. Their importance cannot be overemphasized.

In Years 7, 8 and 9, Form Tutors undertook these reviews with small groups of children at a time from their Form Group, and at these reviews the half-termly progress reports would be considered, together with examination results and attendance data. The focus of these reviews was progress and achievement, and their effectiveness was enhanced because the data to support the review process was available, accessible and easily to hand for each pupil, their parents and the Form Tutors.

Each Year 10 pupil had three individual reviews during the year with the Form Tutor, which again were informed by a range of pupil progress and achievement data together with compact targets which were drawn upon. It was in Year 11 that the crucial difference was made. Twice during the year the school would close for a day so that all staff could be freed to take part in formal one-to-one academic reviews with Year 11 pupils. Before each of these reviews, a self-review sheet was sent to the home of every Year 11 pupil for parents and children to work through together prior to the academic review. The first review was in the run-up to the half-way stage in the year in January, when each Year 11 pupil attended a twenty-minute interview at school with a member of staff. At this interview the self-review sheet was analysed, together with the results of the practice or 'mock' exam taken in January. Attendance and other data were also reviewed. At this review session there was a commitment to set targets which had to be met by the second review in April. The school again closed down for the day and Year 11 pupils met with the same reviewer once again. The second self-review exercise was considered at this meeting, alongside an examination of how far the targets set at the first review had been met. At this review meeting, each member of staff would check with the pupils whether they had familiarized themselves with the detailed study skills booklets which each subject had produced, as an aid to revision in individual subjects. The pupils were required to bring to this review a completed study timetable setting out their detailed revision programme, specifying the topics to be revised for each subject and a schedule of dates and times when this revision would be undertaken. Another crucial part of the strategy for Year 11 was that, on three occasions during the year, staff were asked to provide predicted grades for these pupils. At the start of the year, predicted grades were required from staff based on the pupils' Year 10 performance. Predicted grades were then required in time for consideration at the first academic review in January, and again were required in time to inform the second academic review in April. On each of these three occasions, the predictions were turned into points score totals for each pupil, calculated on the basis of eight points for a predicted *A grade down to one point for a G grade. This meant that, at the start of Year 11, each pupil was given a target points score based on National Foundation for Educational Research (NFER) and Year Eleven Information Systems (YELIS, a development of ALIS – advanced level information systems) indicators. For the two reviews, the target points scores were based on the most recent data provided by staff. This enabled the pupil and member of staff at the review interview to consider whether, and if so why, predictions were falling. Strategies to redress the balance were then invoked to enhance current levels of achievement.

Each Form Group was given a points score to aim for which was an aggregate of the individual totals of each member of the form. Furthermore, these form totals fed into a Year 11 points score, which was also calculated and widely publicized. The emphasis was always a positive one, encouraging children to reflect on the predicted grades which staff supplied and to use this data to consider individual progress and the extent of any gap between current performance and predicted performance potential. Forms were never compared against one another, but the data was used to encourage a sense of teamwork and collective endeavour and to reinforce the idea that each individual had their own important role to play in contributing to the form and year totals. Each subject department was required not only to produce subject-specific study skills booklets but to spend time with Year 10 and Year 11 pupils on study skills techniques and revision planning.

An unexpected feature of the drive for improved quality came from a pupil mentoring scheme, devised by one of the deputy headteachers and introduced in 1996. This opportunity was offered to about fifty of the most able Year 11 pupils who appeared to be underachieving. Staff were asked to volunteer to act as mentors who would meet with a group of children who had taken up the offer, at lunch times or after the close of school, once every two weeks. Their job was to discuss study and revision skills, progress with meeting course work deadlines and occasionally interceding in negotiations between a pupil and a member of staff if there were particular difficulties. A one-off payment of £200, to be spent on classroom resources, was made to those fourteen staff members who volunteered to act as mentors on the scheme. As it got underway, the scheme was recognized by other staff to have great benefits and, as a result, twenty additional staff volunteered to take part the following year. This meant the scheme could be extended on a voluntary basis to all pupils in Year 11. In the second year the programme became more structured and preparations to participate in it began at the end of Year 10, with interested pupils formally invited to apply to take part. A contract setting out the responsibilities of mentor and mentee then followed and was signed by the pupil, parents and staff mentor. The agreement included an undertaking for the pupil and the mentor to meet every two weeks throughout the year. In addition there are normally two meetings a year when parents attend – the launch and the close – but mentors must invite parents to come along once a term as well. In total, 138 Year 11 pupils were mentored by thirty-four members of staff and two LEA Advisers.

In order to introduce the scheme to parents, a mentoring evening was held by the school to which pupils and their parents were invited. The evening was well attended, with parents and pupils being introduced to the principles of the mentoring programme. 'Special occasion' evenings were held with staff, parents and pupils to discuss revision techniques, note taking and other important learning skills, while a specific study skills evening was held prior to the practice 'mock' examinations, when staff worked with small groups of pupils and their parents on study and revision techniques. That evening was also well attended, with pupils and parents being extremely appreciative. A final mentoring evening was held just before the GCSE examinations themselves.

Learning Coordinator posts were created and appointed to each Year Group to examine ways of promoting individual student achievement. The Learning Coordinator role is a central one in supporting the drive to raise achievement by being alert to patterns and trends and their causes, gathering data, reinforcing the key messages to staff, pupils and parents, and so on.

The whole thrust behind these strategies was to create a culture in school which was clearly focused on learning and achievement. As one Learning Coordinator said:

> I did a lot of assemblies and things like that where we talked about the points, we talked about it all the time, so we promoted it heavily within the school and we also promoted the fact that if you were down for getting two points and you achieved your two points that was as valuable to the school as if you got 55 points...so if you achieved or got over your target, then that was really important and it gave a sense of purpose, an aim, a goal...a culture of achievement and celebrating that.

In the school entrance hall, displays were mounted showing the Year 11 GCSE target points score broken down into predictions. These were shown as graphs based on average NFER scores and predicted GCSE scores for each Year 11 tutor group, together with an explanation of the points scoring system and help for pupils in interpreting what the graphs meant. The feeling conveyed is that it is not only an individual endeavour to achieve in line with or in excess of predictions, but that it is also a corporate responsibility. The display serves as a public manifestation of the prime concern for raising achievement, and its prominence in the entrance hall alerts the school community and visitors alike to the commitment to this collective priority.

In these various ways, achievement was placed at the heart of the school's mission and was central to teaching and learning. In 1997 the proportion of children achieving five or more A–C grades rose to 26 per cent, an increase of 10 per cent on the previous year, and the second best set of GCSE results in the school's history:

> I believe that the monitoring and target setting scheme which came about as a result of MIPPRA not only brought about improved results but created a school and a year group of children focused on improvement, focused on the academic rather than the pastoral side of school life.
> (Deputy headteacher)

Evaluation

The various elements of the MIPPRA strategy had combined to create a powerful force for improvement. A culture of achievement was evolving and was constantly reinforced by staff in many different ways, for example:

> In assemblies the key messages were reinforced to pupils about achievement and the need for good attendance and punctuality, together with positive attitudes towards learning in order to maximize achievement… letters were sent home to parents in recognition of good or improved progress made by pupils.

Growing familiarity with the use of data helped staff set challenging yet realistic targets for each child. The importance of data was also understood:

> It's not so much the data itself…it's how you then link it to everything else you know about that child – like attendance, behaviour, punctuality, what's going on at home…there's got to be that human element as well, rather than just the hard-edged scores.
> (Learning Coordinator)

Staff appreciated that the SIP initiative interacted with a number of other school initiatives, particularly the positive discipline programme, the drive to improve literacy as one of the curriculum priorities to improve basic skills, and the assessment, recording and reporting systems. The LEA role was deemed to have been very valuable to the school, particularly in the early days in getting the project underway. Specifically, the school valued the contributions of two LEA Advisers, who worked as part of the staff team acting as mentors to Year 11 pupils. They also praised the centrally provided LEA-run in-service sessions on the gathering and analysis of data, the networking sessions with other schools and the conferences which helped to forge links between local schools and facilitate inter-school visiting in order to learn from one another's practice. Participation in national conferences, particularly information about similar initiatives underway in other schools across the country and school improvement research and practice nationally and internationally, was also thought beneficial in giving the school a wider view.

> The LEA widened our horizons, I think, by providing us with outside speakers, by telling us about things that we might have heard about in the *Times Educational Supplement*. The LEA, I think, here, play that role of having a wider sphere of knowledge because we tend to be a little blinkered. But when you work in one school you do tend to have that blinkered approach, you can get very insular.
> (Learning Coordinator)

There was a feeling among staff interviewed that the LEA had performed an important role in culture setting, in creating a drive to move ahead with school improvement across the LEA, and an impetus to achieve enhanced levels of success. The LEA was described as a catalyst, spurring the school onwards, and always alert to the important school-level issues and readily responding with appropriate advice and support when needed.

> The most useful was the weekend away that LEA SIP personnel organized for us – all five of us went…to a series of lectures and seminars, where a great number of ideas were shared and our action plan was considered…The LEA SIP personnel provided the motivation, I suppose in some ways, the catalyst – they brought us together, we shared ideas.
> (Deputy headteacher)

This collegiate approach to raising achievement, together with the offer of advice and support from the LEA, was something which first attracted the school to participating in the SIP. The deputy headteacher spoke of a sense of collegiality across participating schools, and of working together and sharing ideas and an absence of competition or rivalry in the drive to raise levels of achievement. This was part of the culture which the LEA had helped to nurture, namely one of cooperation, sharing and joint ways of working across schools so that pupils might ultimately benefit from the strengthening of best practice in these sorts of ways. This was an important part of the SIP, and an achievement for the LEA in establishing this ethos at the local level when elements of the prevailing wider climate, for example the publication of comparative tables of performance results, were more divisive in many ways.

One important lesson which had been reinforced from the MIPPRA process was the necessity for the school to achieve the right balance of challenge and support for each pupil and to reinforce the positive aspects in order to encourage confident and well-motivated learners. This was an important part of the MIPPRA process and seen as essential for pupils to gain the most benefit from the learning process and to enhance their levels of success. The experience of participating in this SIP had strengthened this key message:

> It comes down to how we celebrate children's achievement and how we challenge them – that was a really useful experience.
>
> (Learning Coordinator)

Project 2: Improving Literacy

One of the whole-school priorities identified in the school development plan was the need to raise achievement. Part of this was through enhancing basic skills, with one target being literacy skills at both Key Stages Three and Four. The Improving Literacy SIP was seen as something to help achieve this aim, particularly developing strategies to translate whole-school policy into classroom practice which would impact on learning. It was agreed that a framework of four theme areas would take this development target forward. These were:

- readability levels and access to text
- worksheets
- key words
- the use of Information and Communications Technology

The theme of readability levels and access to text was aimed at achieving a better match of text reading level to the reading ability of pupils. This would help pupils gain more independence as learners by becoming better able to access text which has been appropriately selected to achieve a closer correspondence with their own reading capabilities. The aim with worksheets was to achieve greater standardization with them across subjects: the way in which worksheets were organized and presented to pupils, the readability levels assumed, the clarity achieved in terms of what was information, instruction, and supplementary work were looked at. The differentiation achieved in terms of meeting a range of different abilities was also addressed.

Key words and phrases formed the centrepiece for subjects and faculties to identify as specific to their own subject area. These were then publicized to students through classroom display material, and reinforced in lessons through creating opportunities for pupils to increase their familiarity with these specific key words and phrases. Faculties were asked to examine the use of information and Communications Technology as a tool for enhancing the development of basic skills and particularly the development of language skills, research and text manipulation, and presentation of work – including use of computer spell checking.

Faculties were required to develop strategies to reflect these theme areas as a way of translating the agreed whole-school policy into practice. They would need to develop their own statements of intent to show how this would be achieved.

The School Improvement Literacy Project team, consisting of staff representing different curriculum areas, identified elements of the Enhancing Basic Skills policy which were to be developed across the curriculum, and one of these was the concept of 'book power'. Research statistics gathered over one term in the school showed the disturbing finding that, whereas across the term Year 7 pupils borrowed 1,200 books from the school Learning Resources Centre library, during the same period Year 8 pupils borrowed only 207 books. This suggested a quite dramatic decline between Year 7 and Year 8, and was one of the reasons which led to the selection of Year 8 as the focus for the drive to develop book power. The main vehicle for this was the 'book in a bag' initiative. Described by the Coordinator for Literacy as a 'roaring success', pupil questionnaires seemed to acknowledge this perception:

> You can learn to read better in a fun way.
>
> (Year 8 girl)
>
> Excellent because it helps me read better.
>
> (Year 8 boy)

Pupils were overwhelmingly in favour of the scheme, perceiving it to have helped improve their reading, while parents, too, were positive about it. The Curriculum Project Manager noted:

> Since its launch, the 'book in a bag' initiative has been really successful. A book in a bag just encourages them to take a reading book with them at all times...we felt it was a necessary boost to reading and it certainly seems to have paid dividends.

Essentially, the scheme was a way to encourage Year 8 pupils to read, to want to read, and to enjoy reading. Each Year 8 pupil was allowed to choose an attractive drawstring bag in which to keep their reading book, which they had to bring to school every day for the timetabled fifteen minutes daily of silent reading time. Each day, in the first lesson of the afternoon immediately after lunch, there would be a fifteen-minute silent reading period for every Year 8 pupil, with their teachers also encouraged to take out a reading book of their own and share in this activity with the children. Each Year 8 pupil had an attractively illustrated reading card to record details. Each reading book was recorded, together with brief summaries of their favourite and least favourite parts of the book; their own star rating; and their overall response to the book.

Having read the book and completed the reading card, each child would have the opportunity to pull out a prize from the mouth of 'The Mad Book Monster', a decorated box containing popular prizes such as school merits, light refreshment vouchers to be redeemed in the school canteen, cinema tickets and money vouchers. The school purchased many new paperback books which would appeal to this age group, in order to make the scheme popular, and a number of Year 8 pupils helped in the selection of these. The SIP Coordinator for Literacy noted that early evaluation evidence indicated improvements in the reading ability and progress of Year 8 children and that 'Pupils are really, really beginning to want to read. We seem to be creating a habit, which is wonderful!' The previous SIP Coordinator for Literacy also remarked that 'Book in a bag has been a big success with teachers as well':

> A lot of the teachers came up to me and said 'What a great idea!' because it helps them...it's a great start to Period 4 because they've had three lessons in the morning, generally they're tired in the afternoon, they've all been out playing football or whatever else they've been doing...it has a calming effect.

The key words initiative was equally as successful. When faculties were asked which of the four themes they wished to pursue first, most opted for the key words strategy, and a great deal of progress was made. Pupils kept lists of subject-specific key words and phrases, and there were key word displays mounted in classrooms, while teachers encouraged pupils to read and use them as part of learning in the classroom. In Year 11, the key words strategy focused on GCSE exams and the wording of examination questions. The previous SIP Coordinator for Literacy explained:

> If you spoke to kids two years ago to ask them what 'key words' were, they wouldn't know. But now every teacher has incorporated the words 'key word' into their vocabulary, so now the kids know that they need to focus on learning set words and they know the reason why they have to learn them because – mathematics is an excellent example – they might have the mathematical skills...but if they don't have the ability to understand the question then they are going to get the answer wrong, and it's as simple as that.

The school reappraised how information technology was being used to develop literacy skills. From this there was a shared view that staff needed to encourage children to improve the way they used the information they had accessed from a CD-ROM or through the Internet. As the previous SIP Coordinator for Literacy said:

Improving Quality Through a Productive Partnership

When the kids researched information they would just print the information off and hand it in, without necessarily reading it, so that the only actual skill was looking up the information...we were trying to say that perhaps the next stage would be for the kids to highlight the important bits...we've got to be aware that we don't want them just churning out chunks of information.

Many other initiatives formed part of the whole-school approach to literacy development. Examples include a paired reading scheme through which Year 10 pupils acted as reading mentors to slower readers in Year 7, and a school Book Week during which visitors were invited to bring a selection of their favourite books with them and to share readings from these with groups of children.

Evaluation

The SIP Coordinator for Literacy felt that the literacy project had injected a new lease of life and a whole range of valuable ideas into the school. It had 'started something going', creating a momentum of its own which had become 'self-propelling' and so 'igniting a will for the school to improve literacy'. It had also been successful because it had the active support of department heads, who were key players in the process of developing strategies to translate the school policy into practical action which would impact on children's learning:

> Right from the start with this project we found all our heads of departments were with us, you know; this was seen as an initiative that was important, not as just yet another one for them to grapple with, and they have always supported the project, which is why it has been so successful so far.
> (Curriculum Project Manager)

The school felt that the project was also enhanced through the support lent by the LEA:

> I think we've been lucky because I think the Enhancing Literacy project is the one that they've helped the most with. I think that with enhancing literacy, its the right time to be doing it, it fits in with government strategy and it fits in with people's current thinking and we've managed to plug into this. So I think that in that sense the programmes that they [the LEA] are putting together are very thoughtful and do respond to schools' needs... They are there to help people if you want it, the support's there which I think is important. There's a recognition that schools to some extent know what they're doing – they support where

needed, rather than interfere. I think that's a really good policy to promote and I think that they've done that really well.

(Curriculum Project Manager)

The various elements of the project were each deemed to have had many gains and benefits to the school, particularly the SIP conferences which provided new ideas, inspiration and the opportunity to learn from others:

It was exactly what I expected from a conference. It had ideas, it had the experience of other teachers, there was a really friendly atmosphere so I actually quite enjoyed being there socially, and I think it gave you a real 'pick-me-up', because you know...in teaching as a profession you get a lot of knockbacks...and for me personally it was a big enthusiasm booster...Out of the people I've ever heard talking, probably the best speakers I've ever heard have been on the SIPs conferences...It's like a good INSET. It is a boost, and it is 'here's an idea, go away and try it'.

(Previous SIP Coordinator for Literacy)

Things the school SIP team have picked up at those conferences have been excellent – quality speakers – and again its helped us to keep the project moving, keep it alive, to introduce things that have really caught on.

(Curriculum Project Manager)

Other members of the school project team were equally enthusiastic about the different elements of the LEA support. Opportunities to hear about initiatives being pursued in other schools were valued and the active exchanging of ideas and strategies at SIP network meetings was described as enjoyable and useful. The practical focus of speakers at the conferences was welcomed, especially where there were examples of improvement initiatives that had not only consisted of worthy ideas but had made a difference to learning. One project team member made the point that school improvement projects must be more than 'just a lot of people with a lot of ideas'; instead, they must link to learning and pupil performance in order to have validity.

The LEA was also seen to have played an important role in keeping the school from straying from its improvement targets:

It's quite a good idea to have a central figure keeping you ticking along, keeping you focused and pushing you in the right direction...you really do need to keep focused and to keep on task, otherwise it just goes by the wayside.

(Previous SIP Coordinator for Literacy)

REFLECTIONS UPON PRODUCTIVE PARTNERSHIPS

A characteristic of these School Improvement Projects was that responsibility for their operation rested with the schools themselves. The very variety of the projects indicates this point. Moreover, it was accepted by both parties that the LEA needed to respond in many different ways in order for the projects to be effective. The philosophical basis of the relationship was important to its success. In tackling the development agenda, the LEA supported schools in ways which included:

- challenging schools to surpass previous achievements in order to move from strength to strength
- injecting rigour into the process of development
- commending, acclaiming and providing opportunities for schools to disseminate that which has proved worthy
- making available a range of purposeful and targeted support strategies to meet particular and individual school needs

The perception of one of the staff at Rising Dale secondary school regarding the effectiveness of LEA support was that:

> They are there to help people if you want it, the support's there which I think is important. There's a recognition that schools to some extent know what they're doing – they support where needed, rather than interfere. I think that's a really good policy to promote and I think that they've done that really well.

In this particular LEA there is a specific strategy to support school improvement. According to the schools themselves, this support function can be seen as instrumental in providing challenge to attain ever-higher standards of success, while at the same time prompting the schools to stay on course and not stray from pursuit of core purposes. This function is an especially valuable one in times of such turbulence and change, when the prevailing 'task culture' which is so concerned with 'getting things done' can mean that schools are tossed and turned by the forces of change and thus inevitably stray from the course that they have plotted for their own future direction. Quality is to do with seeing things through. Planned and sustained improvement efforts, which are carefully and thoroughly monitored and evaluated, must not be displaced after some short while by other demands and imperatives. Such tenacity is essential, retaining a clear focus on improvement and keeping to task. Schools recognized that, where other pressures have meant that there was a danger of deviating from the improvement targets, the LEA had usefully acted as 'prompter', encouraging them to remain focused on the core tasks. Chadwick Infants, for example, made the point that:

> ...sometimes when you start things off, other things take over...Because the LEA is there behind you, guiding you...it keeps you constantly reminded of what you are focusing on. I think that is a big plus from the LEA.

Applying pressure can be necessary if the temptation of 'ticking along at our own pace' is to be avoided. This pressure in the case of St Andrew's, for example, took the form of the LEA adviser asking difficult and challenging questions, encouraging the school to rethink aspects of its practice and to be more self-critical. This rigorous external scrutiny was welcomed by the school as a valued part of LEA support for school improvement. The contribution made by the LEA to the effectiveness of the action planning at Wideacre Primary was acknowledged by the staff there. At the same time, the headteacher felt that more pressure in the form of greater challenge from the LEA would have acted as a further spur to improvement:

> I would have liked some more pressure because we could have done more, I think. I would have liked somebody to challenge...

This pressure and challenge is important if schools are not to be content with current performance but to realize that, if they are to serve children well, there is always more that can be accomplished. Chadwick Infants invoked the metaphor of a journey on which we are travelling when we embark on the process of improvement, the journey itself being a valuable learning experience and an opportunity to develop new skills and refine ways of thinking. St Andrew's Primary School recognized that the SIP had imposed a discipline on the school which had been useful:

> It was a really good vehicle for us...it has given us a plan and a timescale to do it in, so we've been a lot more 'on task' through being in the project than if we'd just done it ourselves...

This had helped to move the school forward. The 'robustly challenging' (DfEE, 1998a) nature of the LEA approach was considered important in keeping the schools 'on task', and, in the case of Wideacre Primary, had the challenge proved rather more robust, the school felt that rather more might have been accomplished.

An important part of the LEA support role recognized by schools was the help and expert guidance they received at the beginning of the process. This helped in constructing the SIP action plan, and the LEA offered professional advice throughout the SIP. St Andrew's Primary, for example, commented on the benefits from LEA expertise:

> It's their expertise as well...we tend only to see what's going on here... they can share with us suggestions of things that might work and suggestions of things that we hadn't thought of.

The main benefit may be the contribution which the SIP makes to embedding the processes of improvement within the schools' ways of operating. A point made by Wideacre Primary was:

> by doing the project you will actually learn about a process, and eventually you will drop the 'project' bit and you will adopt a school improvement process.

This is the lasting legacy of the School Improvement Projects, and can be seen as a counter-defence against accusations of artificially time-limited projects concerned with effecting improvement. Once embedded within the schools, the focus on improvement becomes part of the established ways of thinking, working and approaching change. If, through participating in a SIP, the capacity and capabilities to develop quality through all aspects of the school's operations is nurtured and enhanced, then these benefits will endure beyond the project itself and have lasting value. Rising Dale Secondary, for example, saw the interconnected nature of improvement tasks it set itself in the ways in which maximizing achievement interacted with other school development priorities. Examples are: behaviour and discipline; monitoring and assessment of pupil progress and reporting to parents; and developments in approaches to teaching and learning. Wideacre Primary School focused on the value of an improvement process which was integral to all that the school accomplished:

> In the end, there never was a project – it became everything – from the word go it was everything. I had this philosophical problem from the beginning with the word 'project' – this is why I found it really difficult to actually tell people what our project was because it never was a single project. We, from the word go, realized it was a process.

A similar point was made at Teesdale Primary School, where the project at first was seen as an 'add-on'. This perception soon changed:

> I felt at first, 'Oh no, its something else we've got to do, its sort of on top of everything else'...But actually as it's gone on and quite soon after we got involved, I began to see that it was part of the Development Plan – it was actually what we might be doing anyway – but it was just a method of carrying it through really...so it's integrated into what we're doing rather than you're doing all your work then you've got to do this extra bit.

The projects helped a refocusing on improvement as a core purpose of schools' teaching, learning and achievement, and this must be at the heart of any drive to develop quality. Effective school improvement can be seen in the development of teachers' skills and expertise, for example in:

- the confidence and capability gained in gathering, analysing, interpreting and acting on data
- the development of the skills of classroom observation and monitoring children's work
- refining the techniques of action planning, target setting, curriculum planning
- extending the range of teaching and learning strategies employed
- finding ways of entering into closer working partnerships with parents and, in the case of Wideacre, with governors too

In these and other ways, the SIP process had prompted senior management and staff in the schools to become more reflective as practitioners. It had encouraged collaborative team approaches and ways of working. It provided a stimulus which had focused staff on school improvement as a key concern, and prompted teachers to talk regularly about and to consider, in more informed ways, the core tasks of teaching, learning and achievement. It had brought rigour and discipline to the approaches taken in the tasks of development and change. The SIP process clearly illustrates the way in which development can be generated from within. St Andrew's Primary School drew attention to the impact of the SIP on the development of the quality of teaching and learning, reporting that:

> There have been improvements in the teaching, what is being taught and how it is taught as well.

Involvement in the SIP had served to challenge existing thinking and practice and had brought with it access to a range of LEA support, including conferences organized by the LEA which in turn fed into and stimulated further development activity. Involvement in the SIP had also helped to influence school culture; for example, at Rising Dale Secondary it was felt that the SIP strategies helped to refocus the school on improvement. This became an important part of the school climate at Rising Dale, creating a drive and a will to improve success, defined by the school as a 'culture of achievement', and making this a collective priority for staff, pupils and their parents.

One benefit of engaging in a SIP is the way in which this can develop the internal capacity of the school to change and develop. This is something which endures beyond the lifespan of any discrete 'project', as Wideacre Primary School found. Through engagement in that process, mastery of

Improving Quality Through a Productive Partnership

many skills and abilities has been gained by schools. This has led to many benefits, including an enhanced potential to develop the quality of teaching and learning and to improve standards of achievement. Hopkins, Ainscow and West (1994, p. 3) have made this point well:

> We regard school improvement as a distinct approach to educational change that enhances student outcomes as well as strengthening the school's capacity for managing change. In this sense school improvement is about raising student achievement through focusing on the teaching–learning process and the conditions which support it. It is about strategies for improving the school's capacity for providing quality education in times of change, rather than blindly accepting the edicts of centralized policies, and striving to implement these directives uncritically.

Engagement in a SIP brought with it reinforcement of the value of the initiatives being pursued and encouragement to continue:

> It actually makes you feel good about what you're doing because you think, hang on a minute, here am I at this little school…and there's people of international reputations coming to talk to us about improvement, and you feel part of something much bigger and also it raises the status of what you're doing.
>
> (Wideacre Primary)

What is clear from these schools' experiences is that the initiative, ownership and direction of the improvement work lay exclusively with the schools themselves. The School Improvement Projects were seen as a vehicle to help meet the schools' own development programmes in more planned and disciplined ways and with the benefits of access to a range of valuable support from the LEA. In particular, support for the construction of the SIP action plan was one valued aspect.

The schools praised the collegiality and teamwork which the SIP had inspired and strengthened in the schools. *Excellence in Schools* (DfEE, 1997a, pp. 27, 28) tells us that:

> The main responsibility for raising standards lies with the schools themselves. Good schools can and should take responsibility for their own improvement…

The SIP experience is about harnessing an internal energy and a desire to effect improvements within the schools themselves. The School Improvement Projects provided a disciplined framework within which to pursue improvement strategies, and a range of support to strengthen the internal capabilities of the schools to effect improvement. The case studies illustrate the best

Improving Quality Through a Productive Partnership

endeavours of professionally competent and confident staff committed to self-improvement and aided by the expertise of LEA officers offering support and validation from an external perspective.

7 Using Problem Solving for Quality Development
Embedding and Sustaining the Process

> Knowledge, therefore, does not simply represent the truth of what is, but rather represents what is taken to be true. Thus taking changes in knowledge as the progressive unfolding of truth, it is necessary to examine the complex exercise of power which is immanent in such changes.
>
> (Usher and Edwards, 1994, pp. 87–8)

This chapter looks at ways of using practical problem solving and techniques to embed and sustain the quality process. The weakness of many reforms is that they lose their power of influence soon after implementation, the drive and energy of reform and continuous quality improvement not being retained. A major problem is to seek ways to sustain such endeavours, and this chapter addresses some of the techniques to enable schools to do so. Methods adopted in one LEA region and its schools were outlined in Chapter 6. Discussed here is the general approach to the issue of how quality is debated and considered in the ordinary school or college, which does not expect to find itself buffeted by a full-scale row or investigation in the near future, but which nevertheless needs to keep a wary eye open for a change of course in the educational world.

There are a number of ways in which problems occur. Some are puzzles – where the solution is there but needs finding. Others are real problems – which may not have a solution or may have one that is outside the usual scope of the problem owner. A puzzle-type problem can be solved by an imaginative study of the constraints upon a timetable, while the problem of structuring to meet budget restrictions from outside is an example of the second form of problem. There are a number of approaches to problems, and they can provide opportunities for the development of quality while involving the members of staff in the exercise.

The quality image is important for any school or college. It must be nurtured. Staff need to be aware of its importance at all times. There is never a time in business when staff can call their product mean and low, and expect to get no reaction to such statements. The chain of Ratner jewellery stores is a famous case in point. Similarly for schools, every report in the local press should be positive. Those schools which address this need seem to benefit from a positive image created among their customers and clients.

Research and development approaches are needed to set a style to which potential customers can relate over a long period of time. Things change slowly in the educational world – there is no overnight sudden pre-eminence of an institution. These things take time to sink into the subconscious of the important decision makers. To think that this is not a process which may affect people in their term of office, however, is wrong. Stages of development need to be stressed, while emphasizing the importance of planned improvement including good design processes to be incorporated at all stages of change.

Conventional approaches to problem solving are generally based on the discovery that 'something is wrong'. Perhaps the coverage of an important event in the life of the school has not been taken up by the local press, while complaints by one or two parents have been publicized instead. The action taken has to be speedy. Consultation with those available, or those normally responsible, is the routine approach. These people then define a solution based on information acquired which inevitably reflects the limitations of their own enquiries. Often a directive is issued, usually in general terms but derived from this specific incident. A sense of relief is thus generated with the assumption that this and all similar problems are solved, and life can return to 'normal' again.

Such an approach will no longer work, because expectations of active problem solving have been raised. Effective problem solving needs, if possible, to be approached in advance. Some of the major constraints on effective problem solving need to be addressed, and among these are time, the random nature of problems, the general lack of resources to tackle problems these days and changes in the situation and nature of the problem during the initial stages of response. The lack of skills of investigation and analysis, and the failure to define resources available, are other major issues. The pattern of life in education, with its gentle rhythm of the academic year, has insulated teachers against the problems of the market-place. However, it is vital that education is responsive in the modern world, and organized problem solving is one way in which this can be developed.

Time is perhaps the major constraint on problem solving. Schools reasonably set a priority on teaching which inhibits giving attention to what are seen as ancillary matters. However, unless senior and middle management devise a system to solve problems, then an effective solution can be more damaging to teaching than the use of time spent on structured problem solving. The random nature of problems is their nuisance value. Problems do not arise at planned intervals, and in real life they intrude on the organized dynamics of the school. However, some may be filtered out by a colleague system which shares power and responsibility to take decisions

Using Problem Solving for Quality Development

at the levels of intended actions, encouraging a rational–empirical approach to management, and operating on an open, accepted 'model'.

A specific or even a general lack of resources, lack of access to resources or a lack of skill in using channels to resources, will interfere with the movement towards the solution. For example, collecting the necessary information can be prevented by the lack of availability of sources of information at that particular time. There may be changes in the situation and nature of the problem during the initial stages of response, and the person taking responsibility for the process may lack the necessary skills of investigation.

Finally there may be a lack of an existing procedure for dealing with the occurrence, where the school system is being overwhelmed with routine administration. Here there is a need to identify established groups of staff who have:

- a relationship
- an effective procedure
- access to the rest of the system
- a responsibility within the area of the problem

In essence, a flexible framework must be created within which problems can be handled as they arise.

How do we best find out where any problems may develop and the ways we may adapt to tackling these? There are a number of avenues to take, and the astute operator accepts all information from a number of sources, bearing in mind the purpose to which the information is to be put. No information is reliable, valid or accurate all the time. Some pieces of data are subject to greater fluctuation from a mean value than others. If a number of sources point in the same direction at the same time, however, then it is wise to take account of the potential impact of that risk to the business of the school. In this way the management will be forewarned and forearmed in the coming struggle – if indeed it materializes as such. Even if it does not, then the experience is a learning curve for the time that other influences will come to bear on the smooth running of the enterprise.

Surveys, audits, panels, observation and experiments all have their own part to play in providing evidence. Surveys offer a first-hand example of thoughts on matters identified as important by the school, but the views of Gunnar Myrdal (1944), who wrote that the way people respond to moral questions depends upon the assumed values of the general society, are valid here. Audits, of course, are more reliable, because the counting of units is a more perfect activity. In questions of quality in education, though, there may be some confusion as to what exactly is being counted. This demands a careful defining of the units concerned before the counting and assessing takes place. In many cases this is a simple factor of agreement between the powerful parties and those who are to provide the counting. For example,

Using Problem Solving for Quality Development

the degree of unapproved absence from a school is currently given a high priority in UK schools, so it is audited precisely, and reasons for absence are listed as approved or otherwise dependent upon the criteria adopted by the central government or LEA.

Panels of interested parties – often known today as focus groups – are a medium relied upon for measuring variations and changes in opinions from time to time. Accurately devised groups are brought together to determine their views as customers on a number of purchase choices. This text argues strongly that there are customers and clients in education, just as in the world at large, so the use of panels of experts or at least representative people is a new way of determining the pulse of whatever changes happen in the environment of the school. Interested parents and those who are seen as opinion formers make up the more representative samples, and they will be advised of possible or potential changes beforehand and asked for their views in confidence before any decision is taken on these issues. This has the benefit of not committing the school to expensive changes that are not seen as beneficial to the wellbeing of the students, their parents or prospective employers – depending upon the subject of the survey.

Such techniques provide evidence upon the perceived effectiveness of education, but do not provide a way of managing a quality response. Before the current programmes were introduced under the National Qualification for Headteachers, the North West Regional Management Centre developed courses for prospective headteachers, and set out a list of competencies for success. The list is not exhaustive, but it provides a challenging outline for any organization seeking to manage quality education (Hoy, 1991), and was used by the Cheshire Educational Management Project.

Competencies Required By School Leaders

Vision

- ability to seek goals and desire appropriate objectives for the school
- ability to perform beyond the immediate needs of the situation
- ability to predict the need for appropriate tasks
- producing original, expressive or imaginative responses to identified tasks
- ability to demonstrate an awareness of value dimensions and preparedness to challenge assumptions

Planning Skills

- ability to plan forward to meet a target
- ability to judge a range of alternative strategies before implementing a plan

- ability to be aware of appropriate timescales
- ability to prioritize
- ability to analyse into discrete elements
- ability to develop detailed and logically sequenced plans to accomplish goals

Critical Thinking

- ability to think analytically and systematically
- ability to apply concepts and principles
- ability to differentiate between routine and analytical thinking

Leadership Skills

- ability to direct the actions of others towards an agreed goal
- structuring interaction to the purposes at hand
- arranging the effective deployment of resources
- willingness to accept responsibility:
    - for the actions of others
    - for achievement of goals
- ability to act decisively in appropriate situations

Persistence

- prepared to make use of a range of strategies to achieve a problem solution
- ability to demonstrate a commitment to task completion
- ability to recognize when circumstances require a flexible response

Influencing Skills

- ability to have an impact on others by action or example
- ability to get others involved in the processes of management
- persuading staff to balance individual needs and institutional requirements
- persuading others to consider a wide range of options

Interpersonal Relationships

- ability to establish and maintain positive relationships
- ability to perceive the needs, concerns and personal circumstances of others

- ability to recognize and resolve conflict
- ability to use effective listening skills
- ability to notice, interpret and respond to non-verbal behaviour
- ability to make effective use of a range of oral and written communication skills
- ability to give appropriate feedback in a sensitive manner

Self-confidence

- ability to feel assured about personal ability and judgment
- ability to demonstrate assertive behaviour without generating hostility
- ability to seek and accept feedback about personal performance and management style
- ability to offer a challenge to others in order to enhance their self-confidence
- ability to offer sensitive feedback to others to promote self-confidence

Development

- ability to actively find ways of enhancing self-knowledge
- ability to demonstrate an understanding of learning style in self and others
- ability to actively seek opportunities to enhance growth in self and others
- ability to assess development needs
- ability to design, implement and evaluate development programmes
- ability to implement a positive climate conducive to growth and development

Empathy

- ability to demonstrate awareness of:
    - the needs of a group
    - the needs of an individual
- ability to listen and communicate in a constructive manner
- ability to indicate sensitivity to the implications of decisions (for others)

Stress Tolerance

- ability to demonstrate appropriate behaviour in stressful circumstances
- ability to demonstrate resilience in pressure situations
- ability to remain effective in a range of working situations
- ability to maintain a balance between priorities
- ability to take into account levels of stress in others

It can well be argued that collecting this data and developing competencies to manage effectively do not help organizations to deal with problems. They do, however, provide a foundation upon which to build. This building can be strengthened by structured use of in-service days. Simulations can be entertaining and provide real opportunities for all to learn. We do not advocate turning schools into experimental laboratories, but suggest that learning organizations need to set up ways in which they can respond to problems and changes organically. One way of doing this is by simulation based upon real problems that are recognized by the staff involved in the training.

A problem arises when there is any discrepancy between an actual situation and an ideal situation which cannot be solved by direct, reflective action. Any task will produce a succession of interactive, or related problems with managers as 'problem-solvers'. Forward looking management will start solving problems before they become crises because these principles are recognized as important axioms on which to base decisions.

Problems can be puzzles or areas of conflict without an immediate obvious outcome or solution; they can usefully be identified in terms of categories of function and field within education, as shown in Table 7.1.

Table 7.1 Categories of function and field within education

Functions	*Fields*
Setting goals	Intra-personal
Designing processes	Inter-personal
Describing roles	Intra-group
Clarifying communications	Between education and society
Improving meetings	
Making decisions	
Designing training	
Reviewing and evaluation	

Indeed, problems are usually multi-faceted, because they are multi-dimensional, and so will point to multiple solutions. There is, then, the possibility of tackling these by setting up problem solving groups; for example, it is widely recognized that there are important changes in career patterns in schooling as a career occupation, with consequent effects on staff attitudes to their present jobs. Similar issues concern the curriculum, teaching styles, assessment, evaluation and accountability, and external relations. For an embattled or complacent colleague, the selection of, and working on, such an issue can be a powerful motivator and an effective morale booster – staff feel they are doing something and hence getting somewhere.

It is a useful idea for managers to establish the idea of multi-dimensional problems, and consequently of multiple, interactive or related solutions. This builds-in the expectation that there is a need for cross-sectional problem solving groups, able to bring in outsiders on an occasional basis. A useful process would be as follows:

- analyse the problem for its different levels and aspects
- seek information internally and externally
- approach the problem on several of the points where it exists
- involve at an early stage the original informants of the problem
- be prepared to split the group into smaller task groups to reconvene at frequent and regular intervals to review, coordinate and plan the next set of sub-tasks for the full group to consider

Essential aspects of planned problem solving are differentiation and integration – allowing the system to generate alternative ideas based on different but complementary functions which nevertheless draw everything together into an overall strategy.

It is impossible to see problem solving for quality improvement as a single-issue or fixed-time process towards a solution. Problem solving is continuous because no solution is either absolute or final. Solving the problem of improving relationships with students and employers is likely to create another one: for example, how to find and programme the necessary time.

It may be useful to adopt a model set of questions, such as the one shown in Table 7.2, to address all problems.

We argue that this approach can be used effectively by applying a paradigm (Hoy and Wood, 1993) for developing targets for continued quality enhancement. We suggest that a picture can be drawn up to show where a group wants to be (see Figure 7.1).

To use the paradigm effectively, certain definitions need to be applied. Aims are an ideal towards which you are striving, often given as a generalized statement with some assumption that changes may be necessary along

Table 7.2 Model set of questions to address problems

Where are we now?	This will involve a description and analysis of the current situation.
Where do we want to be?	This will require a description and analysis of the hoped-for target to be identified. If we don't know where we are going, then any road will do.
How can we get there?	This will identify, describe and state the implications of a number of paths or solutions.
How will we know when we've arrived?	This assumes that the aims, goals and objectives of the process have been agreed beforehand, so that recognized evaluative outcomes can be identified.

the path to the achievement of those aims. Aims are referenced to values and experiences, they affect the whole organization and are long-term ends which define the choice of goals and objectives. Using the convention that one evaluates a course or programme, and assesses the course participants on that programme, then some form of evaluation should accompany aims, while an assessment is made of goals or objectives.

Goals are an actual destination, an attempt to operationalize the aim; they are a product of analysis of an aim describing intermediate, medium-term stages, are referenced to practice and refer to a set of activities, functions or specific tasks within an organization. They define more closely the choice of objectives, but also contribute towards the achievement of aims. They relate to assessment more than to evaluation.

Objectives are specific operational statements, short-term targets. Stated clearly in realistic terms, they will map out individual steps to the achievement of the goals. They are often associated with behavioural activities, and will state conditions and criteria.

Once a problem has been defined and recognized, and the constraining and driving forces related to solutions analysed, then an action plan can be designed. Again a planned approach is important. An approach along the commonsense lines shown in Table 7.3 could be adopted.

Once the plan is in place, implementation should not be delayed, and periodic review dates should be agreed while keeping open channels for feedback. There is nothing new or revolutionary in this planned approach to dealing with problems. We believe that quality development can only occur and continue in any organization when the foundations upon which it rests are carefully laid by people who feel involved in the process.

There are many techniques that can be used to help the process of group problem solving along. We put forward two for consideration: the Synectics

Figure 7.1 Problem solving paradigm

```
              theory  -->  practice   =>  resources

Aims            0           0              0              Strategic

Goals           0           0              0              Tactical

Objectives      0           0              0              Operational


              ought  <-->  can      <=  time/effort
```

process, and one offering a focus upon opportunity finding rather than problem solving.

The Synectics Process

The basic approach of Synectics (Borden, 1960) is to listen, to take offers on their merit, but to defer decisions on approaches to the solution. One valuable technique in Synectics is that of ditch jumping. This is a planning process using techniques of 'accept' or 'reject' and 'question' or 'offer'. This is reinforced through the importance of checking with the owner of the problem the progress being made at all times.

Working with the second of Michael Fullan's (Fullan with Stiegelbanner, 1991) ten assumptions (referred to in Chapter 4), there arises the issue of

Table 7.3 Problem solving action plan

What?	Choose the brainstormed ideas which seem best.
Who?	Decide what group or persons should expedite them.
How?	List the materials/resources likely to be needed.
	Put the ideas and actions into a time sequence.
	Plan the beginning of the sequence as soon as possible.
When?	Estimate specific dates for particular actions to occur.
	Make plans for commencing the action sequences.
How will you know?	Make plans to evaluate periodically the effectiveness of the actions as they are implemented by stating indicators and criteria.
How will you modify/adapt?	Be prepared to revise the plans as the sequence unfolds.

Using Problem Solving for Quality Development

how best to discuss a problem which is mentioned by a colleague. One useful way to solve the issue is to consider the problem through the Synectics method of learning-by-doing.

The discussion group takes the problem, which can be expressed either as a puzzle, a wish or the unravelling of a complex situation in the search for a new solution. In many cases this is accompanied by a need for conflict resolution – the 'people' side of the problem. The 'problem owner' volunteers the problem for resolution. The group decides how to conduct the discussion for the problem to be noted and acted upon, and appoints one member as the 'facilitator' or 'chair' to ensure the discussion moves on to possible generation of a solution. The group discusses offers of suggestions to address the issue, and the meeting is then analysed by the facilitator in terms of whether an interjection was a 'question'. The facilitator paraphrases it to be questioned by the problem owner, and the process continues towards resolution. Such a process requires a number of items to be accepted:

1   Concentration on the intent behind the question. Members of the group continue to listen, to paraphrase the question and seek for the intent behind the question from the questioner.
2   A memory of what the original problem/issue was. A taking back to the beginning with the challenge to offer three types of solutions.
3   Time to work through the solutions produced so that there is no rush to a quick fix solution. The ditch-jumping process is one way of working through a problem or issue.

Ditch jumping allows the group to 'rescue' an individual who has fallen into a trap or problem by building a ladder to success from the depth of the hole, rather than permitting the individual to remain in the hole – or even to keep on digging it deeper. It can be represented as shown in Figure 7.2.

The purpose of using Synectics is to help a person trapped in the ditch to climb out. They can do this by using a ladder lowered down to them by the members of the group. In this way, offer leads to offer, and so by helping each other share the problem and its solution a clearer outline of the problem arises in the minds of all members of the group.

Synectics offers a focus on the initial conditions that make for innovative solutions. It allows us to begin to focus on how we can move forward. The process will move the problem owner on from the beginning, 'building' by slowly shifting along possible routes to solutions applicable to that person. Major errors occur when 'problem solvers' attempt to leap in to reach the end point (see Figure 7.3).

It is in fact possible to start at any point in the process, as long as there is building towards the solution. However, members of the group must always check with the problem owner that progress is being accepted. If the group believes that insufficient progress is being, then the Synectics method

Using Problem Solving for Quality Development

Figure 7.2 Ditch jumping

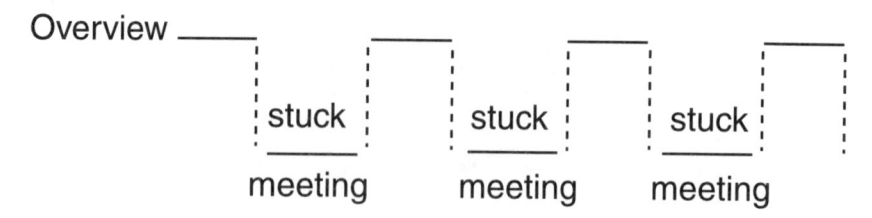

Overview ── ┌╌╌╌╌┐ ── ┌╌╌╌╌┐ ── ┌╌╌╌╌┐ ──
　　　　　　 ┊stuck┊　 ┊stuck┊　 ┊stuck┊
　　　　　　 └╌╌╌╌┘　　└╌╌╌╌┘　　└╌╌╌╌┘
　　　　　　 meeting　　meeting　　meeting

Figure 7.3 Solution finding

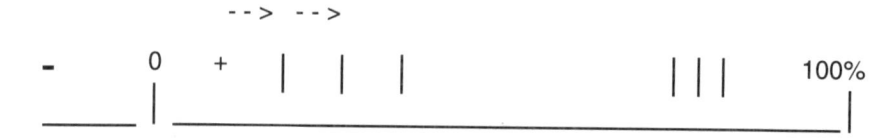

```
            -->  -->
   -    0  +  |  |  |              |  |  |    100%
   ____|_____|
```

requires that a break from solution hunting is made. Instead, in a second session there is what is termed an excursion from direct problem solving. The problem is put to one side, and something different is undertaken, together with the purpose of building up the experience as a team. A third session can then return to the problem solving.

A focus on opportunity finding rather than problem solving

While there is a need to address potential solutions to everyday problems encountered in schools, it is in seeking out opportunities that progress lies. Rather than repeating the corrective action to return to the status quo, the course that problem solving implies, there are more beneficial alternatives if a rational and planned search is undertaken for opportunities that may be available for quality enhancement. The opportunity finding process differs from, but is built upon, standard problem solving approaches. It is therefore useful to revisit that process first and then turn attention to the opportunity finding extensions to it. The aim is to distinguish between different phases in the processes of decision making, and to apply problem solving techniques to everyday decisions.

Decision making describes the process through which a course of action is selected as the solution to a specific problem. Choice making and problem solving are different activities: choice making refers to the narrow set of activities involved in choosing one option from a set of alternative options, and is therefore but one part of decision making. Problem solving refers to the broad set of activities involved in finding and implementing a course of action to correct an unsatisfactory situation. Problem finding refers to the

Using Problem Solving for Quality Development

process of identifying a problem and making the decision to attempt to solve it.

Problem finding, choice making, decision making and problem solving are five separate but related stages, as shown in Table 7.4.

Types of problems and decisions

Programmed decisions Those that are made in accordance with some habit, rule or procedure. Routine decisions are not necessarily simple ones. To some extent programmed decisions limit our freedom, because the organization rather than the individual decides what to do. However, programmed decisions are intended to be liberating. It might help to think of examples of such programmed decisions, and those which, in your opinion, ought not to be programmed decisions.

Non-programmed decisions Those that deal with unique or unusual problems. It is these decisions that the trained manager meets more often, and for which training in how to make decisions reasonably is given.

For example, you may wish to think about the last major decision you were called upon to make, as part of your own job, which you found hard to make. How did you go about solving it? Were there any lessons to learn from that experience? Did you learn them? What advice will you give yourself next time?

Examples of both programmed and non-programmed decisions are given in Table 7.5.

Decision making techniques

In the area of non-programmed decisions, managers can find opportunities to plan quality development if they adopt planned processes in problem solving. By harnessing the mind power of all involved in a school, it should

Table 7.4 Decision making

← Decision making →				
Activities dealing with determining the existence and importance of problems	Activities dealing with identifying defining, and diagnosing problems	Activities dealing with generating alternative solutions	Activities dealing with evaluating and choosing among alternatives	Activities dealing with implementing the chosen solution
Problem finding			Choice making	
← Problem solving →				

Using Problem Solving for Quality Development

Table 7.5 Programmed and non-programmed decisions

Types of decisions	Traditional	Modern
Programmed:		
Routine, repetitive decisions Organization develops specific processes for handling them	Habit, clerical routine Standard operating procedures Organization structure Common expectations A system of sub-goals and well-defined information channels	Operations research Mathematical analysis Models Computer simulation Electronic data processing
Non-programmed:		
One off, ill-structured novel policy decisions Handled by general problem solving processes	Judgment, intuition and creativity Rules of thumb Selection and training of executives	Heuristic problem-solving techniques applied to: a) training human decision makers b) constructing heuristic computer programs

be possible to take advantage of situations presented as problems to exploit opportunities.

Crisis decisions are usually triggered by a sudden single event: something requires immediate attention. Problems become apparent through a stream of ambiguous and frequently verbal data, stimulated by the accumulation of multiple events. Opportunities, on the other hand, are often evoked by an idea or a single non-crisis event.

An enormous amount of research has been devoted to problem solving, whereas a very small amount examines problem finding, and even less examines opportunity finding. However, opportunities rather than problems are the key to organizational and management success. Solving a problem merely restores normality, whereas it is the exploitation of opportunities which produces results.

Opportunity finding means seeking ways to release talent so that creativity, productivity and quality enhancement come together. Opportunity is not a fixed entity, but on a scale which starts from satisfactory and progresses through good to promising and on to excellent, opportunity can be identified as the point at which brilliance lies. The gap between good work, excellent quality and the brilliance of new opportunities can be very wide indeed. The scope for developing schools to reflect the excellence we know they already possess, and going on to perform brilliantly, is at the core of the opportunity finding process.

One way to identify this route is through comparative studies in education, and, within that route, to explore the problem approach first used by Brian Holmes in *Problems in Education: A Comparative Approach* (1965).

This bore the fruit of Sir Karl Popper's (1945) concepts of critical dualism from his approach in *The Open Society and its Enemies*, as modified by Nicholas Hans (1958). Brian Holmes set out his philosophy in his inaugural lecture as professor at the University of London Institute of Education (Holmes, 1979). This was directed towards identifying general statements about specific initial conditions from which a known prognosis may legitimately be deduced. For Holmes:

> The scientist regards either the generalization or statements about initial conditions as problematic. His interest is in testing the prognosis from statements by comparing predicted outcomes with observable events.

From our perspective, this helps, but the opportunity seeker needs to go further than to:

> formulate alternative policies, describing the conditions under which they are to be introduced, and deciding which of the alternative policies is most likely to work by eliminating the others.

The need is to move from problem solving to regain of the status quo towards new opportunities as solutions.

Nicholas Hans (1958) believed that national education systems were an outward expression of national character, but was unable to substantiate these feelings, despite his attempts to classify factors which have influenced educational development. His assertion that, because of the variety of forms in which data are found, statistical comparisons have little value, would leave a lot to be desired in educational quality measurements in the contemporary world. This gap, however, had already been filled by John Dewey and the American pragmatist school of educational development.

There are two methods of argument. 'Induction' means arguing from the particular to the general, while 'deduction' is arguing from the general to the particular. Although induction cannot be a logically rigorous process, nor can it lead with certainty to new discoveries, Medawar (1969) is of the opinion that most original research begins with a Baconian, that is an inductive, experimentation, but that inductivism confuses the process of discovery and of justification. By contrast, for Medawar, a sound methodology must provide an adequate theory of special incentive – a reason for making one observation rather than another, a restrictive clause that limits observation to something smaller than the universe of observables. In looking for opportunities, this will help us immediately in identifying something to be imaginative about, and will later on provide a background of observation and experimentation before any exploratory dialogue can begin. This 'something to be imaginative about' defines the domain of facts in an initial survey of the situation. So, although Medawar favours the adoption of the hypothetico-deductive mode of arguing for the scientific method, he still maintains a place for induction. It is a careful tuning of this inductive process that will lead to opportunity finding.

This chapter provides an excursion into the ways any school can embed quality development into its life. The intention is not to provide prescription, but rather to stimulate thinking. As Peter Drucker (1979, p. 387; see also Drucker, 1992) advised: 'Doing the right thing is more important than doing things right.' The pursuit of quality is the aim, and we put forward some ways in which this search can be helped along.

It might be argued that the most important variable in problem solving is the element of time. What amount of time can be devoted to solution searching, opportunity finding, Synectics approaches to cooperative actions and the like will depend upon the way any given amount of time is spent. It is therefore very instructive for all people involved in looking for quality enhancement to address the inevitable overloading of time. One approach or another is essential for the operation to be encountered and overcome in the space of time that the individual has available.

With this point in mind, this chapter concludes with twelve fingerposts pointing to principles of effective time management:

1 Say YES with enthusiasm to a request or activity that will contribute to the completion of important work, but say NO, nicely, when important work will be affected badly.
2 Concentrate on important work first. Delay is the major enemy of productivity.
3 Control work stress by identifying, confronting and eliminating the source of the stress.
4 Analyse what needs to be achieved in a job by clarifying and setting job objectives, then schedule important work ahead.
5 Be positive and flexible about work activity, planning ahead in order to balance the time for reaction and that for planned activity.
6 Manage priorities by understanding their nature and managing ahead in order to avoid potential priority conflicts.
7 Control your time and your diary by making sure that time is available for scheduling important work.
8 Develop teams with an emphasis on priorities, direction, involvement and harmony.
9 Plan and control meetings with an emphasis on action and time.
10 Carefully plan and brief work that has to be delegated and then ensure follow-up.
11 Meet with support, administration and secretarial staff to involve them effectively in the teamwork.

12 Be ruthless and quick with routine duties and paperwork, using the best technologies to support your personal organization.

These twelve fingerposts point the way ahead for all workable efforts to enhance the quality of education in schools.

8 Quality: the Search for the Holy Grail of Organizational Development

'Why,' said the Dodo, 'the best way to explain it is to do it.' (And, as you might like to try the thing yourself, some winter-day, I will tell you how the Dodo managed it.)

First it marked out a race-course, in a sort of circle, ('the exact shape doesn't matter', it said) and then all the party were placed along the course, here and there. There was no 'one, two, three and away!', but they began running when they liked, so that it was not easy to know when the race was over. However, when they had been running half an hour or so, and were quite dry again, the Dodo suddenly called out 'The race is over!' and they all crowded round it, panting, and asking 'But who has won?'

(Lewis Carroll, *Alice's Adventures in Wonderland*)

The Caucus-race described in *Alice's Adventures in Wonderland* was an unconventional race in which not only did all the participants emerge as winners but also the purpose of getting dry was achieved. Furthermore, the Dodo said firmly that the best way to explain things is to do them. We suggest that the present approach to quality development put forward by central government is to regard the race as straight, with clear winners and losers, when in fact it is much more complicated.

We also argue that the present framework will not sustain quality development. The time has come to reconsider and provide a framework that will encourage schools to pursue improvement and quality development. As Ted Wragg and Tim Brighouse (1995) wrote of OFSTED:

The present framework for inspection, even in its simplified form, is not a proper means of improving teaching and learning. It produces mechanical reports, written to a formula dominated by national averages, expressed in language that would be used in no other educational context. Implicit within it is the assumption that improvement is brought about by shaming teachers.

Quality: The Search for the Holy Grail

With these words and those of the Dodo ringing in our ears it is time to reconsider the nature of the race. If the purpose of the Caucus-race was to get dry, then the purpose of the education business must be to provide quality teaching and learning. The crucial question must be the way in which this can be done.

Six propositions for managing change can be adapted from Fullan (Fullan with Stiegelbanner, 1991):

1 All large scale change is ultimately *implemented locally*.
2 Change is *learning* – loaded with uncertainty.
3 Change is a *journey*, not a blueprint.
4 Change is *resource hungry*.
5 *Seeking assistance* is a sign of intelligence.
6 Change requires *power to manage*.

What we have tried to show in this text is that the decision to value our own motivation, and the motivation and drive of all with whom we work, is essential to carry us forward in the cause of improving the quality of education. Successful change and quality development depends essentially on the integrating of personal and organizational goals. Only through the goodwill, perseverance and dedication of the staff will the management vision be put into context in the planned improvements in quality demanded in today's world of education. All need help to do that, and continued professional development is by its very nature the way most schools enhance the capabilities of their staff members.

Staff development and training is a process of matching future requirements, as identified by the objectives and business plan, with the current performance of the individual staff, as identified through the development review process. It can be described in diagrammatic form, shown in Figure 8.1.

The business plan identifies future requirements into three areas: high (Hi), medium (M) or low (Lo). The current performance delivered by individuals – or the sections or departments in which they currently work – is similarly classified as Hi, M or Lo.

The decision has then to be made as to whether resources should be devoted in a concentrated way on those elements of the business that are performing excellently now and are expected to continue to do so in the future – thus improving the effectiveness of the organization, or determining whether some effort is going to be needed in those areas that are currently performing well but where future growth cannot be guaranteed. At the low end of the matrix, questions have to be asked. Planned withdrawal is a difficult concept for schools, but in higher education there is currently a debate as to whether or not certain institutions should concentrate upon certain subjects, and 'specialist' schools in the secondary sector are being created.

The evidence from schools is clear, as the case studies considered in

Quality: The Search for the Holy Grail

Figure 8.1 Staff development and training

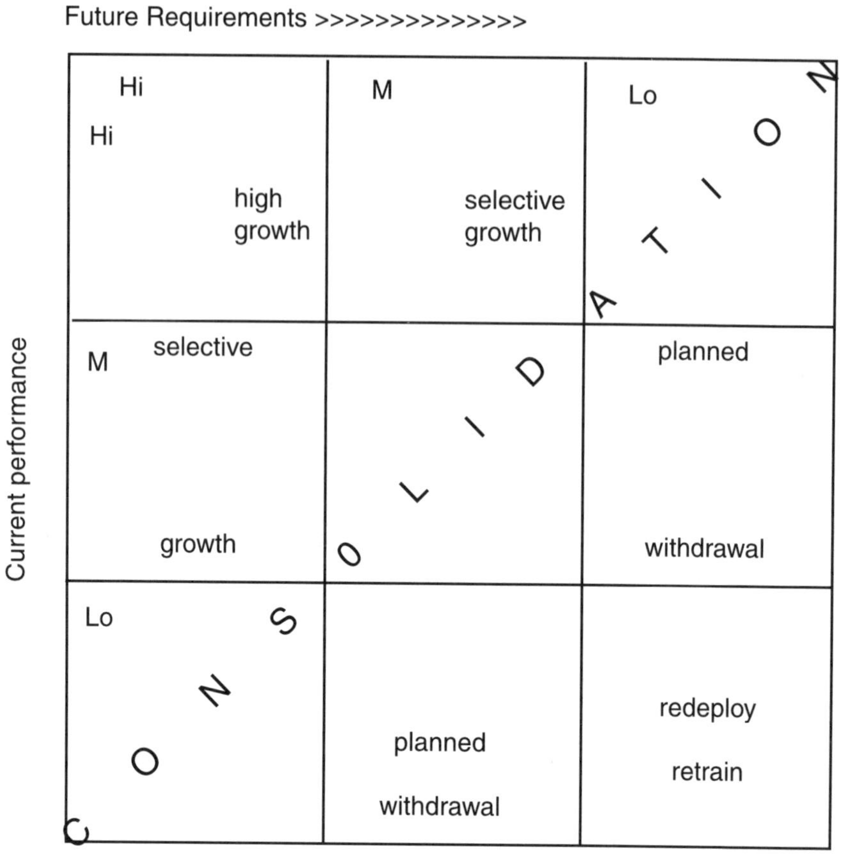

Future Requirements >>>>>>>>>>>>>

	Hi	M	Lo
Hi	high growth	selective growth	
M	selective growth		planned withdrawal
Lo		planned withdrawal	redeploy retrain

Current performance (y-axis)

NOT AN OPTIONS (diagonal annotation)

Chapter 6 illustrate; as does the Schools Make a Difference Project (Myers, 1996). Schools can manage their own improvement and develop a sense of collective awareness if they are given appropriate resources and encouraged to improve on their previous best. They have to make decisions as to the best way in which to deal with their own weaknesses.

Motivating staff is a vital aspect of such school-based development. Collaborative planning and implementation fit Herzberg's (1966) motivators and hygiene factors. Schools that permit and encourage teachers to exercise more autonomy in making decisions, to take more individual responsibility in developing and implementing teaching programmes and to develop professional skills, are more likely to produce a high positive level of teacher satisfaction and commitment, and a positive correlation between teacher attitude and pupil performance.

William Glasser (1990), in his book *The Quality School*, argues powerfully for what he terms 'lead-management' rather than 'boss-management' in schools. He states that the quality of work will increase under lead-management 'because the workers and the managers are working together much better than before'. It is important to remember that any change in schools is a socially negotiated process. Coercion will not provide the collaborative atmosphere in which such negotiation can take place. Inspection is currently viewed as a tool of the boss-manager and, as such, will not unlock a school's potential. Valerie Hall (1996) suggests that school leaders can create conditions in which a school becomes a learning organization. Such leaders have been described as 'post-heroic' (Seashore Lewis, 1994). They delegate and empower colleagues; they encourage teachers to invent solutions to problems and are not the only problem solver; they can leave the school without everything falling apart.

There is little in organizational development that has not been tried in one form or another in the past. This is certainly true in relation to the current phase of School Improvement Officers, just as it was the innovative actions of the advisory teachers in the 1980s that produced such a useful development in realistic terms for schools – well before the era of improvement through inspection returned to haunt the educational scene. However, bearing in mind the need to focus on the classroom, the laboratory and the lecture hall in the search for quality education, we believe that there should be a shift to managed school development powered from within the school. Within our definition of the customer the school is the place where quality development will be generated.

Collaborative work has to be planned. Groups of teachers will require the following (O'Shea, 1990):

- clearly scheduled time for meeting and discussion
- training in group processes including chairmanship
- strategies and skills for decision making
- procedures for regular communication to those not immediately involved
- setting of realistic targets
- ability to persevere under pressure
- agreement to work with and learn from the group process itself

Once groups are formed with a purpose, then things must be made to happen. We would advocate dealing with matters in bite-size chunks. 'Chunking' is a process advocated by both Peters and Waterman (1982) and Goodchild and Holly (1989) – get one's arms round a problem so that it can be manipulated effectively and work in task groups to sort things out. It is a sensible approach to problem solving.

The small group is the most visible of the chunking devices. Small groups are, quite simply, the basic organizational building blocks of excellent companies. Usually when we think of organizational building blocks, we focus on higher levels of agglomeration – departments, divisions, or strategic business units. Those are the ones that appear on the organization charts. But in our minds, the small group is critical to effective organizational functioning....Teams that consist of volunteers, are of limited duration and set their own goals are usually found to be much more productive than those with the obverse traits.

(Peters and Waterman, 1982)

Focus, fluidity and flexibility are the three words to keep in mind while setting up task groups to tackle issues of quality and development in a school. The task is demanding and rewarding, but it is vital to draw upon the expertise of all involved if the quality of the process is to be improved. As Deming (1982) stated in his fourteenth point:

> Put everybody in the company to work to accomplish the transformation. The transformation is everybody's job.

As we have tried to show in this text, motivation to achieve success is an important feature of quality. The degree of motivation will vary from person to person, and will be dependent on the perception the person has of the particular task ahead. However, according to McClelland (1961), some 10 per cent of the population have a specific need to achieve in a highly developed form. This need applies to a general level of motivation, if certain criteria are fulfilled in the work that they are asked to undertake. An example can be seen from one of the case schools in particular. Wideacre Primary School was led by a headteacher with a vision and a strategy to move the school towards the realization of that vision. He used the results of his stakeholder survey to inform that vision and the construction of development targets. The School Improvement Project was one of the strategies used to realize one of the overarching aims – to raise achievement through more effective management of the curriculum.

Those who set out to achieve a particular standard in their work should be identified and used to provide models for others. McClelland (1961) believes these tendencies emerge at a very early age, and continue into adulthood. It is worthwhile for schools, colleges and universities to try to recruit such highly motivated individuals, and set them tasks which will enhance the achievement of the school. High-need achievers, according to Everard and Morris (1996, p. 27), are likely to be drawn to managerial positions or to work as independent entrepreneurs. It goes without saying that among people with similar levels of ability it will be those who have a strong need to achieve who are motivated to succeed, and will deliver the best quality outcomes for the organization.

McClelland's studies have identified three major characteristics of the self-motivated achiever. Everard and Morris say that, because of these characteristics, many of the usual supervisory procedures are likely to prove inappropriate in their case.

First, high-need achievers like to set their own goals. Being driven by such an in-built motivatory factor, they are always trying to influence life or to make things happen instead of merely letting things happen to them. Being quite selective about which goals they set themselves, they are unlikely to take readily to goals set entirely by others – including their line managers.

Second, high-need achievers tend to avoid selecting goals which are extremely difficult to achieve. They prefer tasks which challenge their abilities, but which are achievable by their own efforts and which will respond to their determination to overcome, rather than merely succumb by chance actions. High-need achievers prefer tasks which will provide them with immediate feedback, including measurements of how they are doing towards solving the problems they have selected for themselves.

Third, high-need achievers prefer tasks which provide them with rapid feedback. They need to know how much progress they are making towards their goals, because these goals are extremely important for them to achieve. If managers can give more immediate indication that these high-need achievers are moving towards their own individual goals, then the better they perform. It is the managers' responsibility to ensure that these individual goals relate accurately to the goals of the organization.

This defines the Holy Grail. The task is to get school managers to see how to unite all in a common task of improving quality in their schools.

Further research in this area of motivation and how best it can be harnessed to enhance quality in schools is long overdue. The exciting opportunities of exploring ways to achieve greater motivation for certain approaches to improving quality can be expected in future, using McClelland's investigations applied to school improvement. The discovery by McClelland that monetary incentives are actually more effective with people whose achievement drives are relatively weak, because they need some kind of external reward to increase their effort, ought to be thought through by school managers. The really effective way to enhance quality, then, is through recognition and praise, rather than monetary reward. The Further Education Funding Council (FEFC) has recognized this in its recent proposal to invite high-performance colleges to apply for a special status. Higher education is to be similarly treated in the next round of Quality Assurance Agency proposals, where much greater reliance on the internal processes of review will be all that excites the outside agencies. Not all is cosy, however, as the FEFC appears to be saying that it will use the resources released from the current whole-college grading inspection to focus on the 10 per cent of 'failing colleges'. The FEFC still has far to go to learn the folly of its prognostications, but the colleges will in future have to judge themselves more acutely on criteria such as student retention and achievement. It is a step in the right direction, though early estimates suggest that only one college in five is expected to gain accreditation.

A similar opportunity was awarded by the Council for National Academic Awards to those elite group of institutions soon to become the fledgling New 1992 Universities through its Partnership Agreements on accreditation. The key is to build more achievement characteristics into the job. Precisely the opposite has been happening under OFSTED inspection methodologies. There is a need to highlight personal responsibilities and individual participation in the selection of targets. Again, this runs counter to the current fashion of controlled curriculum, detailed procedures and requirements. The setting of moderate goals and fast, clear feedback of the results is what is required instead. General guidance and occasional follow-up will suffice as supervision for high-need achievers. Internal feedback is an essential feature of success.

This is best delivered by precise, detailed, honest opinions of how people are performing with their tasks. These people need to be managed in a different way from existing methods if the best improvement in quality is to be gained from them. As we have been reminded by many authorities, to be educated is not to have arrived at a destination, but to travel with a different view. Part of that view is the necessary and sufficient requirement for all to contribute to the enhancement of quality, whatever their ability, on a continued basis. There have been many managers of the education system. Thoughts about how to organize it change from age to age. The hope now is that the self-developing and self-managing school will provide better-quality enhancement than any inspection programme can ever provide.

What we have discovered in the writing of this text is that the concept of quality is still ill-defined, that there is much confusion over the meaning of the word 'quality', in education and other publicly provided service sectors. It is clear that the effects of inspection on quality enhancement are largely negative instead of positive, and that only the efforts of all engaged in the education service working together to their own established agendas, along with the help of other outside bodies, can assist in the renewal process being put into place over a longer period of time than an annual inspection round. Progress to improving quality in education has to be continually revisited. There needs to be constant development from within the schools, colleges and university departments through validated self-review processes. These rightly need to be standardized and audited, but that is a far cry from the physical inspection process which operates as a first-line interrogation. What is required is an adaptation of the public enquiry approach into an event in which the public has a distinct and definite interest, except that this has to be institutionalized into a continual process – not an external examiner's visit once a year or a quality assessment once every three years or so. Where the organization can go wrong in its move towards improving quality in education is through adopting a rigid approach focused on minutiae while missing the larger goal. In the same way a diffuse concern and reporting procedures will do equal harm to the process. Where the two ends of this continuum need to come together is in the determination, the motivation, to strive continually to improve. That is the essence of the process, with everyone engaged throughout the year – not just for one week or so of exhaustion to meet standards that should have been integrated into the work of the teams throughout the process. It is the mindset that is different in this latter approach. Constant appeal to better performance from those who can label an institution as 'failing' can only dispirit the inmates further. The motivation to succeed is within the powers of the teams that make up every responsible aspect of the school.

Improving quality through a productive partnership is certainly one valid and proven way forward. The role of the LEA as critical friend and confidant was well established in the past – augmented with the collaboration of Her Majesty's Inspectorate as the eyes and ears of the Ministry of Education. They were certainly not the prescribers and limiters of acceptable practice. Far from it; they passed on hints and ideas to motivate other like-minded or complacent staff in other schools, and they did it almost subconsciously and effectively.

How can we reinvigorate the motivation for all in schools to succeed? Perhaps a further summary of the effects from the case study and an analysis of the motivation engendered there will suffice to end the arguments as to ways forward in at least the cases that matter. Periodic, formal, structured academic reviews were at the heart of the strategy of success for the secondary school in the case study. Their importance cannot be overemphasized. At Wideacre Primary School the headteacher took a very proactive stance in leading whole-school development and was aware of the need to gain the commitment of stakeholders. He did this by consulting teachers, parents and governors to establish an understanding of their perceptions of the school's strengths and weaknesses, and then by using this data to inform the process of establishing development priorities. Personal motivation was at the forefront of these developments. Again, in the secondary field, Learning Coordinator posts were created and appointed in each Year Group to examine ways of promoting individual student achievement.

Of course there still remains the question of outside support and accountability to the clients. Accountability is simply addressed. There is a plethora of bodies that audit the work of education. A slimmed-down inspection framework could be used to audit the work of schools and license them to undertake their own reviews of their own action plans.

The next issue is the way in which appropriate support is provided and encouragement for schools to learn from each other is given. There is a real danger that central government could export the crisis over funding of education to schools by placing education in the hands of school governors and capping local authorities. Schools would become islands and thus isolated (Brennan, 1993).

We would argue that any organization needs assistance as it sets out on its journey towards quality and improvement on its previous best. The assistance could well be tied into the allocation of resources. In the Hereford and Worcester evaluation programme of the Technical and Vocational Enterprise Initiative (TVEI) extension developments, 'evaluation was not seen as something "tacked on" to education development, but as integral to it'. It was essentially a formative part of the progress of the project. The project carried resources with it to the schools involved, and the use of the resources was evaluated under the guidance of Professor Gleeson of Keele University by local evaluators – TVEI curriculum development staff – and by internal evaluators – the teachers and senior managers in the schools. There were some reservations about the amount of evaluation, and a 'squirm' factor was apparent as a result of suspicion about the motives of the evaluators (Gleeson et. al, 1994). The project, however, empowered schools, and it was felt that the evaluation had provided valuable learning opportunities. There are bound to be tensions between schools managing their development and central funding initiatives. These tensions can be resolved as this project demonstrated. Accountability within an agreed conceptual framework is possible without external control of the specific developments.

The external support needed for any development can thus be used to ensure accountability while acting as a mentor or critical friend. These support agents generate self-evaluation in the form of joint reflection (Bayne-Jardine and Holly, 1994). Ed Bambrough (1992) has this view:

> If the advisory service can provide a viable service in the shape of advice, guidance, help, counselling, development and training, utilising a wide range of skills and encompassing a support network...then schools under Local Management may well call on their expertise.

Organizations need 'another pair of eyes' to help them see their way ahead in their search for quality, but this is not a controlling role. Advisers should be seen as partners working with staff to promote good practice and quality development.

There is little value in terms of the overall effect of quality improvement if only certain individuals are attached to institutional development. Greater value comes from a team approach to performance management and direction. This necessitates a sharing of the needs of the institution, seen best through common aims, goals and objectives for the whole system, and then making the performance management process fit these needs. The most usual method is development, and action planning moves forward in line with an agreed business plan.

We have advocated task groups working with a focus to enact development plans and improve on previous best. Outside involvement is best retained in the 'critical friend' role. Eisner (1985) makes the point that teachers are too close, and a critical friend provides a fresh eye, distance and an illuminative intent. The process is not quite coaching; rather it is more the counsel of friends. Trust is vital, and people only make themselves vulnerable to those who they believe intend no harm. The very word 'inspector' can strike dread into the most confident teacher's heart. Reason takes a back seat in the atmosphere of pre-OFSTED pressures. Joint reflection on the process of learning rests on the investment of time in the classroom and an integrated programme of professional development. The role can be played by members of a school's staff working with colleagues, with an external critical friend to ask questions about the school-based process. There is no set pattern for such review. It is a matter for each organization as to the best way to check their way of working. Portraiture, a picture in words of a school painted by an outsider, can be a powerful way in which we can be helped to see ourselves as others see us (Lightfoot, 1983).

One important role that OFSTED might fulfil would be to act as a court of appeal in the event that there are complaints about the quality of education being provided by a school. It is realistic to plan for a positive way in which to deal with a school that is felt to be underperforming by parents, students, the community or the LEA. It would be necessary to have a mechanism by which an external review could be arranged, because there will be occasions upon which clients and customers consider that validated self-review has gone off the rails. The fact that such a review body exists would reassure those who consider such a system as too cosy. Furthermore, the expertise built up by OFSTED teams could then be utilized appropriately.

OFSTED could also carry out a national strategy for research. David Hargreaves, in the 1996 Teacher Training Agency lecture, has argued for 'a new partnership between researchers and practitioners'. Such a partnership must be fostered and the work coordinated. He suggests a National Educational Research Forum should set the course for research. OFSTED now has built up a huge database, and this resource must be used to inform research into methods of developing quality in schools.

The recent demand by central government for quality assurance has made an impact, and much has been learned – not least that inspection on its own does not bring about improvement. Senge (1990) suggests that people learn most rapidly when they have a genuine sense of responsibility for their actions. The theme of this book is that schools in the broad sense of that term should be given back the responsibility for improvement. In this way, learning matters, because it lies in the hands of the teachers themselves. Schools as learning organizations embark on a journey that has no end, and those in the schools are living beings, not pieces in a jigsaw puzzle. A living organization grows from within, and it is vital that schools are encouraged to solve their own problems for the purpose of empowering students to learn.

It must, of course, be remembered that schools are quirky and idiosyncratic institutions. The micropolitics of school organization have been described as an 'organizational underworld' which all recognise and in which all participate. Unless this dimension of any school is understood and harnessed, school improvement will not take root. Surely the moment has come when school leadership provided by headteachers, principals, department heads and governors should be trusted to manage in the interests of quality education. This is a daunting task, and managing the micropolitical pressures in any institution is, in our view, rendered almost impossible when outsiders constantly interfere. After all, in the words of a Royal Secretary to King Charles I: 'There goes more to it than the bidding it be done.'

References

Allen, Roger E. (1995) *Winnie-the-Pooh on Management*. London: Methuen.

Audit Commission for Local Authorities in England and Wales (1989) *Assuring Quality in Education: a report on Local Education Authority Inspections*. London: HMSO.

Bambrough, E. (1992) 'Advisers – can we afford them?', in Lowe, P. (ed.) *The LEA Adviser and Inspector* pp. 120–32. London: Longman.

Bayne-Jardine, C.C. and Holly, P.J. (eds) (1994) *Developing Quality Schools*. London: Falmer Press.

Beeby, C.E. (1966) *The Quality of Education in Developing Countries*. London: Oxford University Press.

Beeby, C.E. (1967) 'Planning and the educational administrator'. *Fundamentals of Educational Planning*, no. 4, p. 19. Unesco Institute for Education. Paris: UNESCO.

Belbin, R.M. (1981) *Management Teams: Why they succeed or Fail*. London: Heinemann.

Bennett, N. and Galton, M. (1976) *Teaching Styles and Pupils' Progress*. London: Open Books.

Berger, P. and Luckmann, T. (1967) *The Social Construction of Reality*. London: Allen Lane.

Birmingham City Council (1992) *Quality Development Resource Pack*. Birmingham: Martineau Education Centre.

Bolam, R. (ed.) (1982) *School Focussed In-service Training*. London: Heinemann.

Borden, W.J.J. (1960) 'Synectics', quoted in Nolen, V. (1990) *The Innovator's Handbook*. London: Sphere Books.

Brennan, M. (1993) 'Reinventing Square Wheels: Planning for Schools to Ignore Realities', in Smyth, J. *A Socially Critical View of the Self-Managing School*. London: Falmer Press.

Brighouse, T.R.P. (1997) 'From the Bronx to Birmingham', *Times Educational Supplement*, 7 February, p. 19.

Bright, M. (1998) 'School "shame" squads fail exams test', *Observer*, 23 August, p. 16.

Burns, T. and Stalker, G.M. (1961) *The Management of Innovation*. London: Tavistock.

Cliff, P.S., Nuttall, D.L. and McCormick, R. (eds) (1987) *Studies in School Self-evaluation*. Lewes: Falmer Press.

145

References

Collins, J.C. and Porras, J.I. (1997) *Built to Last: Successful Habits of Visionary Companies*. New York: Harper-Collins.
Cowen, R. (ed.). (1996) *The Evaluation of Higher Education Systems*. World Yearbook of Education 1996. London: Kogan Page.
Critten, P.W. (1993) *Investing in People: Towards Corporate Capability*. London: Butterworth-Heinemann.
Davis, A. (1998) 'The limits of educational assessment', *Journal of Philosophy of Education*, March.
Day, C., Whitaker, P. and Johnston, D. (1990) *Managing Primary Schools*. London: Paul Chapman.
de Bono, E. (1970) *Lateral Thinking for Management*. London: McGraw Hill.
Deming, W.E. (1982) *Out of the Crisis*. Cambridge, Mass: MIT Press.
Deming, W.E. (1993) seminar at General Motors, Detroit, 2–4 March.
Deming, W.E. (1994) *The New Economics for Industry, Government, Education*. Cambridge, Mass: MIT Press.
Department For Education (1992a) Education Secretary John Patten's letter to Professor Stewart Sutherland, HM Chief Inspector of Schools, 8 September.
Department For Education (1992b) *Choice and Diversity: a new framework for schools* (Cm 2021). London: HMSO.
Department for Education and Employment (1994) *Improving Schools*. London: OFSTED/HMSO.
Department for Education and Employment (1995a) *The OFSTED Handbook. Part 1: The OFSTED Framework: Inspection Requirements*. London: OFSTED/HMSO.
Department for Education and Employment (1995b) *Planning Improvement: Schools' Post Inspection Action Plans*. London: OFSTED/HMSO.
Department for Education and Employment (1997a) *Excellence in Schools* (Cm 3681). London: The Stationery Office.
Department for Education and Employment (1997b): *LEA Support for School Improvement, a Framework for the Inspection of Local Education Authorities*. London: OFSTED.
Department for Education and Employment (1997c) *Inspection and Re-Inspection of Schools: New requirements and guidance on their implementation*, August 1997, from September 1997.
Department for Education and Employment (1998a) *Code of Practice on LEA–School Relations: Draft for Consultation*. London: DfEE.
Department for Education and Employment (1998b) *School Evaluation Matters*. London: OFSTED.
Drucker, P.F. (1979) *Management* (an abridged and revised version of *Management: Tasks, Responsibilities, Practices*). London: Heinemann-Pan.
Drucker, P.F. (1992) *Managing for the Future*. Oxford: Butterworth-Heinemann.
Dunham, J. (1995) *Developing Effective School Management*. London: Routledge.
Eisner, E.W. (1985) *The Art of Educational Evaluation*. London: Falmer.
Elliott, J. (1981) *School Accountability*. Oxford: Blackwell.
Everard, K.B. and Morris, G. (1996) *Effective School Management*. London: Paul Chapman.
Fullan, M.G. with Stiegelbanner, S. (1991) *The New Meaning of Educational Change*. London: Cassell.
Gabor, A. (1990) *The Man Who Discovered Quality*. New York: Penguin Books.

References

Gardner, H. (1993) *The Unschooled Mind*. London: Fontana.
German, B. (1991) *The Role of the Advisory Teacher: Case Studies in the North West of England*, M Phil thesis (unpublished), University of Manchester.
Glasser, W. (1990) *The Quality School*. New York: Harper Row.
Gleeson, D., Turrell, D. and Russell, V. (1994) 'Undertaking Collaborative Inquiry: Evaluation for a Change: Inside a Development Project', in Bayne-Jardine and Holly (eds), *Developing Quality Schools*, London: Falmer Press.
Goodchild, S.R. and Holly, P. (1989) *Management for Change: The Garth Hill Experience*. London: Falmer Press.
Goodlad, J.I. (ed.) (1987) *The Ecology of School Renewal*. Chicago, Ill.: University of Chicago Press.
Goodlad, S. (1995) *The Quest for Quality: Sixteen forms of heresy in higher education*. Society for Research in Higher Educaction. Buckingham: Open University Press.
Hall, V. (1996) *From Management Self Development to Managed School Development: Issues in School Management Training*. Bristol: Bristol University.
Halpin, A. (1957) 'Administrative theory in education', quoted in Holmes (1965) *Problems in Education*. London: Routledge.
Handy, C.B. (1989) *The Age of Unreason*. London: Business Books.
Hans, N (1958) *Comparative Education: a study of educational factors and traditions*. London: Routledge and Kegan Paul.
Her Majesty's Inspectorate of Schools (1977) *Ten Good Schools*. London: HMSO.
Herzberg, F. (1966) *Work and the Nature of Man*. Cleveland, Ohio: World Publishing Company.
Holly, P. (1986) 'Teaching for learning, learning for teaching', *Curriculum*, vol. 8.
Holmes, B. (1965) *Problems in Education: A Comparative Approach*. London: Routledge.
Holmes, B. (1979) *Ivory Towers, the Glass Bead Game and Open Societies: The social functions of comparative education*. London: University of London Institute of Education.
Holt, M. (1981) *Evaluating the Evaluators*. London: Hodder and Stoughton.
Holt, M. (1987) *Judgement, Planning and Educational Change*. London: Harper and Row.
Holt, M. (1993) 'Dr Deming and the improvement of schooling: no instant pudding', *Journal of Curriculum and Supervision*, Fall.
Hopkins, D. (1987) 'Implications for school improvement at the local level', in Hopkins, D. (ed.) (1987) *Improving the Quality of Schooling: Lessons from the OECD International School Improvement Project*. Lewes: The Falmer Press.
Hopkins, D., Ainscow, M. and West, M. (1994) *School Improvement In an Era of Change*. London: Cassell.
Hoy, C.H. (1984) 'Comparative analysis and its application to multicultural education', in Corner, T. (ed.) *Education in Multicultural Societies*. London: Croom Helm.
Hoy, C.H. (1991) 'The management development centre', in *Management Development Programme*, pp. 21–7). Consortium for Educational Management Development Monograph. Education Management North West, North Cheshire College.

References

Hoy, C.H. (1998) 'Aspects of lifelong learning: symposium', at *The 11th International Congress for School Effectiveness and Improvement*. Manchester University, 4–7 January.

Hoy, C.H. and Gray H. (1992) 'Appraisal and staff development: towards a university solution', *Educational Change and Development*, vol. 12, no. 2, pp. 4–9.

Hoy, C.H., and Race, P. (1996) *Mentoring and Staff Development*. Issues in Staff Development No. 3. Universities and Colleges Staff Development Agency, University of Sheffield.

Hoy, C.H. and Whittle, R. (1988) 'Educational policy for 16–19 year olds: staying or leaving?', *Education Today*, vol. 38, no. 3, pp. 63–7.

Hoy, C.H. and Wood M, (1993) 'Taking charge of change: the ultimate challenge for the school', *Educational Change and Development*, vol. 14, no. 1, pp. 27–33.

Hoyle, E. (1970) 'Planned organizational research in education', *Research in Education*, vol .3.

Institute For Public Policy Relations (1993) *Education: a different vision, an alternative White Paper*. London: IPPR.

Investors in People UK (1996) *Investors in People Standard*. London: IiP.

Kanter, R.M. (1991) 'Change-master skills: What it takes to be creative', in Henry, J. and Walker, D. (eds) *Managing Innovations*, London: Open University and Sage Publications.

Kohn, A. (1992) *No Contest: the case against competition*. Boston: Houghton Mifflin.

Kohn, A. (1993) *Punished by Rewards: the trouble with gold stars, incentive plans, and other bribes*. Boston: Houghton Mifflin.

Kramm, K.E. (1985) 'Improving the mentoring process', *Training and Development*, April, pp 40–2.

Lightfoot, S.L. (1983) *The Good High School*. New York: Basic Books.

Lowenstein, L. (1996) 'Who inspects the inspectors?', *Education Today*, vol. 46, no. 4, p. 48.

MacIntyre, A. (1982) *After Virtue: A study in moral theory*. London: Duckworth.

McClelland, David C. (1961) *The Achieving Society*. Princeton, NJ: Van Norstrand.

Maden, M. and Hillman, J. (1996) 'Lessons in success', in *Success Against the Odds*. National Commission on Education. London: Routledge.

Medawar, P.B. (1969) *Induction and Intuition in Scientific Thought*. London: Methuen.

Morgan, G. (1986) *Images of Organization*. London: Sage.

Morris, G. (1988) 'Applying business consultancy to schools', in Gray, H.L. (ed.) *Management Consultancy in Schools*. London: Cassell.

Mortimore, P. (1998) *The Road to Improvement: Reflections on school effectiveness*. Amsterdam: Swetz and Zeitlinger.

Mullen, P. (1977) *Beginning Philosophy*. London: Edward Arnold.

Murgatroyd, S. and Morgan, C. (1993) *Total Quality Management and the Schools*. Buckingham and Philadelphia: Open University Press.

Myers, K. (1996) *School Improvement in Practice*. London: Falmer Press.

Myrdal, G. (1944) *An American Dilemma*. New York: Harper.

Nagel, E. (1961) *The Structure of Science: Problems in the logic of scientific explanation*. New York: Harcourt and Brace.

Neave, H. (1990) *The Deming Dimension*. Knoxville, Tenn.: SPC Press.

Nichols, A. (1983) *Managing Educational Innovation*. London: Allen and Unwin.

Noah, H.J. and Eckstein, M.A. (1969) *Toward a Science of Comparative Education*. London: Macmillan.

O'Shea, A.T. (1990) *Planning and Implementing School Development*. Department of Education for Northern Ireland, pp.15–19.

P.A. Consulting Group (1992) *The Total Quality Experience: a guide for the continuing journey*. London: PACG.

Peters, T.J. (1987) *Thriving on Chaos*. London: Pan Books.

Peters, T.J. and Waterman, R.H. (1982) *In Search of Excellence: Lessons from America's best-run companies*. New York: Harper and Row.

Popper, K. (1945) *The Open Society and its Enemies*. London: Routledge and Kegan Paul.

Postman, N. (1996) *The End of Education* (video).

Reddin, W.J. (1971) *Managerial Effectiveness*. New York: McGraw-Hill.

Reid, W.A. (1997) 'Conceptions of curriculum and paradigms for research: the case of school effectiveness studies', *Journal of Curriculum and Supervision*, Spring.

Rose, L. and Gallup, A. (1998) '30th Annual Phi Delta Kappa/Gallup poll of the public's attitudes toward the public schools', *Phi Delta Kappa*, September.

Rutter, M., Maugham, B., Mortimore, P. and Ouston, J. (1979) *Fifteen Thousand Hours*. London: Paul Chapman.

Sammons, P., Hillman, J. and Mortimore, P. (1995) *Key Characteristics of Effective Schools*. London: University of London Institute of Education/OFSTED.

Schon, D.A. (1983) *The Reflective Practitioner*. New York: Basic Books.

School Management Task Force (1990) *Developing School Management – the Way Forward*. London: HMSO.

Scottish Consultative Council on the Curriculum (1996) *Teaching for Effective Learning*. Dundee: Scottish CCC.

Seashore Lewis, K. (1994) 'Beyond "managed change": Rethinking how schools improve', in *School Effectiveness and School Improvement*, vol.5, no.1.

Senge, P.M. (1990) *The Fifth Discipline: the art and practice of the learning organization*. London: Century Business.

Senge, P.M. (1994) 'The leader's new work: building learning organisations', in Mabey, C. and Iles, P. (eds), *Managing Learning*. London: Routledge.

Stoll, L. and Myers, K. (eds) (1998) *No Quick Fixes: Perspectives on Schools in Difficulty*. London: Falmer.

Thompson, D. and Reeves, J. (eds) (1947) *The Quality of Education: Methods and purposes in the secondary curriculum*. London: Frederick Muller.

Tysome, T. (1998) 'Quality: How it all fits together', *Times Higher Education Supplement*, 5 June, p. 6.

Usher, R and Edwards, R. (1994) *Postmodernism and Education*. London: Routledge.

Van Vught, F.A. and Westerheijden, D.F. (1994) 'Towards a general model of quality assessment in higher education', *Higher Education*, vol. 28, no. 3, pp. 355–71.

Weick, K. (1985) 'Sources of order in underorganized systems: themes in recent organizational theory', in Lincoln, Y.S. (ed.), *Organizational Theory and Inquiry: the paradigm revolution*. Beverly Hills: Sage.

Wilcox, B. and Gray, J. (1996) *Inspecting Schools*. Buckingham: Open University Press.

Winch, C. (1996) 'Quality and education', *Journal of Philosophy of Education*, March.

References

Wood, M. (1998a) 'Traveller families and schools: round table discussion' at *The 11th International Congress for School Effectiveness and Improvement*. Manchester University, 4–7 January.

Wood, M. (1998b) 'Partners in pursuit of quality: LEA support for school improvement after inspection', in Earley, P. (ed.) *School Improvement after Inspection?* London: Paul Chapman.

Wragg, E.C. and Brighouse, T.R.P. (1995) *A New Model of School Inspection*. Exeter: Exeter University School of Education.

Index

academic reviewers 57
academic reviews 101–2, 141
access to text 106
accountability 4, 14–15, 32–3; support and 141–2
accreditation 68, 139–40
achievement: culture 93; monitoring individual pupil progress to raise 99–106; motivation and 138–40
action 37
action plans: post-OFSTED inspection 28, 55, 82–3; problem solving 125, 126; SIPs 73, 75–6, 83, 91, 94–5
activity/process arena 21–2
adoption and adaptation 53–4
advisers, LEA 79, 80–1, 104, 142; link advisers 66, 72, 75–6, 89, 91–2
advisory teachers 137
aims 15–16, 38, 124–5, 126
Ainscow, M. 115
Allen, R.E. 33
allocation of resources 142
America 2000 programme 9
annual review 83
assessment 6–7, 43
Association of University Teachers 56
Audit Commission for Local Authorities in England and Wales 16–17
audits 23, 119–20; external audit 67–9

Baker, K. 32
Bambrough, E. 142
Baseline Assessment 88
Bayne-Jardine, C.C. 69, 142
'Beacon Schools' 14
Beeby, C.E. 18–19
benchmarking 56, 57
Bennett, N. 43
Birmingham City Council Quality Development Resource Pack 12, 50, 59, 70
Boeing 747 jumbo jet 7
Bolam, R. 29
'book in a bag' initiative 107–8
'book week' 89, 109
Borden, W.J.J. 126
boss-management 136–7
Brennan, M. 142
Brighouse, T. 12, 33, 50, 74, 134
Bright, M. 27
British Quality Foundation 60, 61
built-in quality 13, 31, 38–9, 63
Burns, T. 53
Business Excellence model 60–1
business sponsorship 26
Byers, S. 34–5

capabilities, key 61–2
capacity for change 114–15
Carroll, L. 134
catalytic consultancy 54
central government 16, 21; *see also* Department for Education and Employment
centralized services 26
Chadwick Infants School 86–92; English language development for multi-lingual learners 87–9; evaluation 90–2; LEA support and involvement 89–90
change: capacity for 114–15; managing 30–2, 50–2, 135
change-masters 52–3
Charter Marks 27, 34–9
choice making 128–9
chunking 137–8
clients 10–12
Cliff, P.S. 10

151

Index

coaching 43–4
Codes of Practice 41, 58
Collins, J.C. 3, 7, 8, 9
commitment 37, 42, 95–6; *see also* motivation
Committee of Vice Chancellors and Principals 56
communication 53
comparisons 131
competencies required by school leaders 120–3
competition with oneself 9
conferences, SIP 78, 83–4, 89–90, 97, 104–5, 110
conformity to common standards 40–2
consistency 67
consumerism 13, 29–30
context: local context for quality improvement 72–3
continued professional development 31; development review 40–8, 135, 136
Continuity and Progression SIP 82–3
contract conformance 11–12
control 16–20; changing context 20–3
cooperation 105
corporate status 21
Council for National Academic Awards 140
critical friend 49, 54, 143; development review 43, 47–8; LEA as 33–4, 63–6, 72–3, 141
critical thinking 121
culture: school 85–6, 96–9, 105–6, 113, 114; sharing–learning culture 48
curriculum coordinators 87, 91–2, 95–6, 103, 107, 108, 141
curriculum management 93–5, 97
curriculum planning 82–3
customer-driven quality 11–12
customers 10–12

Davis, A. 5
Day, C. 49
de Bono, E. 49
Dearing Report 56, 57
decision making 128–33; levels 21–2; programmed and non-programmed decisions 129, 130; techniques 129–33
deduction 131
degree awarding 58
Deming, W. Edwards 1–2, 5, 33, 42, 138; built-in quality 31, 38–9, 63; questions 70; and total quality management 3, 36
Deming Cycle 50, 51
Department for Education and Employment (DfEE) 11, 15, 66; *Excellence in Schools* 14, 71, 115; *OFSTED Handbook* 32
development competencies 122
development plans 73, 75, 82–3, 93–4, 95, 142–3
development review 40–8; continuous quality improvement involving all staff 134–44; role of the critical friend 47–8; role of the mentor 44–7
development from within 49–59
Dewey, J. 131
dialogue 32–3; reflective 65
dissemination 83–4, 97
ditch jumping 126, 127, 128
Drucker, P. 132
Dunham, J. 48
dynamism 31

Education Act 1986 16, 20
Education Reform Act 1988 16, 20
educational standards *see* standards
Effective Teaching SIP 76–7
effectiveness, school 5–6, 12
Eisner, E.W. 54, 143
Elliott, J. 69
embedding improvement 85–6, 96–9, 113
empathy 122
employers: as customers 11
enablers 60–1
English language development 87–9
equality 14
Ethnic Minorities Support Service 72
European Foundation for Quality Management 60
European Union 21–2
evaluation 37, 44; productive partnerships 79–81, 84–6, 90–2, 96–9, 104–6, 109–10
Everard, K.B. 138
expertise, LEA 80–1, 104, 112–13
external audit 67–9
external examiners 56, 57
external review 143
extrinsic assessment 6–7

failing schools 40
fields, categories of 123
focus 85

focus groups 120
Ford Motor Company 1–2
form tutors 101
formative assessment 43
Framework for Supporting School Self-Review 64
Fryer Report on Lifelong Learning 33
Fullan, M.G. 26, 50, 126, 135
functions, categories of 123
funding 20–1, 141–2
further education 17, 18, 55, 139–40; changing context 20–1; self-review 66–70
Further Education Funding Council (FEFC) 17, 18, 139–40
future 26

Gabor, A. 1
Gallup, A. 5–6
Galton, M. 43
Gardner, H. 48
Garrick Report 56, 57
GCSE 99, 101–2, 103–4
Glasser, W. 136–7
Gleeson, D. 142
goals 15–16, 125, 126, 139; Investors in People 37–8
good practice 58
Goodchild, S.R. 137–8
Goodlad, J.I. 53
Governing Bodies 20
governors 96, 97
Gray, J. 29, 47
group working 124, 137–8, 142–3
Guidelines for the Review and Internal Development of Schools (GRIDS) 31, 69

Hall, V. 137
Halpin, A. 21
Hamilton, A. 55
Handy, C.B. 47
Hans, N. 131
Hargreaves, D. 143
headteachers: competencies required by 120–3
Hereford and Worcester LEA 69–70
Herzberg, F. 136
high-need achievers 138–40
higher education 17, 18, 28, 34, 41, 139, 140; development from within 55–8; proposed standards in higher education 56–8; validated self-review 66–70
Higher Education Funding Council (HEFC) 17, 18, 27, 28, 34
higher valuations 17
Hillman, J. 12–13, 14
HMI 6, 141
Holly, P. 69, 70, 137–8, 142
Holmes, B. 130–1
Holt, M. 2, 28, 55
home activity pack 88–9
Hopkins, D. 31, 115
Hoy, C.H. 31, 38, 47, 120, 124
Hoyle, E. 53

image 117–18
Impressionism 3
Improving Literacy SIP 106–10
in-service education 123
individual pupil progress, monitoring 99–106
induction 131–2
influencing skills 121
Information and Computer Technology 106, 108–9
information/data 90, 119–20
innovation 25
inspection 27–39, 140; Charter Mark approach 34–9; HMI system 6, 141; improvement and 17, 29–34, 49–50; language of 28–34; snapshot approach 63; *see also* Office for Standards in Education
inspection report statements 17
Institute for Public Policy Relations 32
institutional practice 8–9, 58
interactive communicator 47
interpersonal relationships 121–2
Investors in People (IiP) 27, 34–9

Japanese car industry 1
Jefferson, T. 55
Johnston, D. 49

Kanter, R.M. 52–3, 55
Kenmore School, New York State 74
key capabilities 61–2
key words and phrases 106, 108
Kohn, A. 5
Kramm, K.E. 45

language coordinator 87, 91–2

153

Index

language development 87–9
LEA advisers *see* advisers
lead management 136–7
leadership 15; competencies required by school leaders 120–3
leadership skills 121
learning: continuous by teachers 47–8, 59; dynamic process 50, 51; quality of in higher education 56, 58; self-review and 66
learning coordinators 103, 141
learning organization 31–2, 46–7, 66
Lightfoot, S.L. 47, 54, 143
link advisers 66, 72, 75–6, 89, 91–2
literacy 106–10
literacy coordinator 107, 108
Local Education Authorities (LEAs) 6, 11, 15, 22; and control of education 16–17, 20; as critical friend 33–4, 63–6, 72–3, 141; Hereford and Worcester LEA 69–70; partnership for quality 62–6; productive partnership case study 70–4, 75–116; support 89–90, 98–9, 111–13
local financial delegation 20–1
Local Government Act 1966 Section 11 88
Lowenstein, L. 27, 29
lower valuations 17

McClelland, D.C. 18, 20, 138–9
McCormick, R. 10
MacIntyre, A. 8–9
Maden, M. 12–13, 14
management: arena and control of education 21–2; of change 30–2, 50–2, 135; organic system of 53; school 19
Manpower Services Commission 56
Medawar, P.B. 131–2
mentoring: development review 43–4, 44–7; pupil mentoring scheme 102–3
Minister for Standards in Education 32–3
mission statement 15
model set of questions 124, 125
monitoring 95–6
Monitoring Individual Pupil Progress to Raise Achievement (MIPPRA) project 99–106
Morgan, C. 11–12
Morgan, G. 49
Morris, G. 54, 138

motivation 18, 33, 136, 140–1; high-need achievers 138–40
Mullen, P. 30
multi-dimensional problems 124
multi-lingual learners 87–9
Murgatroyd, S. 11–12
Mustang P51 fighter 2–3
Myers, K. 136
Myrdal, G. 17–18, 119

'naming and shaming' 14, 33, 40, 49–50
National Council for the Inspection of Schools 33
National Curriculum 9
National Educational Research Forum 143
National Higher Education Qualification 57
Neave, H. 5, 50
Needs Assessment Scores 88
network meetings 78, 83, 90, 110
networking, informal 97
newsletters, SIP 90
Nichols, A. 53
non-programmed decisions 129, 130
North American Corporation 2–3
North West Regional Management Centre 120
numerical measures 5, 13, 30
Nuttall, D.L. 10

objectives 15–16, 38, 125, 126
Office for Standards in Education (OFSTED) 15, 37, 54, 61, 140; action plans 28, 55, 82–3; audit model 49–50; conformity 40–1; critique of 134; external assessment process compared with HEFC and FEFC 17, 18; 'Improving Schools' 58; inspecting quality in 27, 28–34; possible roles for 143; quality assurance 11–12; *School Evaluation Matters* 60; SIPs and OFSTED inspections 82–3, 91
opportunity finding 34–5, 128–33; decision making techniques 129–33; types of decisions 129, 130
organic system of management 53
organizational development 134–44
O'Shea, A.T. 137
outcomes: defining quality 15; teaching 25–6
outsourcing 26

P51 Mustang fighter 2–3
P.A. Consulting Group 30
paired reading scheme 109
panels 120
parents 30; involvement in language development 88–9; MIPPRA project 101, 102–3
Partnership Agreements on accreditation 140
partnerships: nature of productive partnerships 111–16; partnerships for quality 15, 62–6; productive 58–9, 75–116, 141
Patten, J. 32
performance data, school 94–5
performance management 42, 142
performance reviews 23
performance targets *see* targets
persistence 121
personal and professional goals 38
Peters, T. 1, 53, 54, 137–8
Phi Delta Kappa/Gallup poll 5–6
planned withdrawal 135, 136
planning: curriculum 82–3; Investors in People initiative 37–8; overall planning of teaching 24–5; SIPs and 75–6, 82–3; skills required by school leaders 120–1; *see also* action plans, development plans
policy aims 38
Popper, K. 131
Porras, J.I. 3, 7, 8, 9
portraiture 47, 54, 143
Postman, N. 5
practice, institutional 8–9, 58
predicted grades 101–2, 103
presentations 83–4, 89–90
pressure, LEA 98–9, 111–12
proactive quality development 30–1
problem finding 128–9
problem solving 34–5, 117–33; opportunity finding 128–33; Synectics process 126–8
problem solving groups 124
problem solving paradigm 124–5, 126
procedure 119
productive partnerships *see* partnerships
programmed decisions 129, 130
progress: monitoring individual pupil progress to raise achievement 99–106
progress reports 101
public interest area 21–2
purpose 4, 12

qualifications 56, 57
quality assurance 3–4, 11–12, 34–5
Quality Assurance Agency 41, 55–8, 68
quality business 10–26; changing context 20–3; complex process 23–6; control of the process 16–20; customers and clients 10–12; development 34–6; quality in the future 26
quality control 34–5
quality development 18–19; validated self-review and 60–2
quality in education 29–30; concept 1–9; defining 10, 12–16; organizational development and 134–44
quality standards *see* standards
quantitative data collection 90
quantitative measures 5, 13, 30
questions: model set of 124, 125; spirit of inquiry 70

Race, P. 47
'Raising achievement through effective curriculum management' SIP 93–5
reactive problem solving 118
reactive quality 30
readability levels 106
Reeves, J. 30
reflective dialogue 65
Reid, W.A. 5
relationships, interpersonal 121–2
renewal 53
research 143; teacher as researcher 48
resources: allocation of 142; problem solving and 119
responsibility 143–4
results: enablers and 60–1
Rising Dale Secondary School 99–110; evaluation 104–6, 109–10; Improving Literacy project 106–10; Monitoring Individual Pupil Progress to Raise Achievement (MIPPRA) project 99–106
Rose, L. 5–6
Russell, V. 142

St Andrew's Primary School 75–81; effective teaching 76–7; evaluation 79–81; SIPs as force for improvement 77–8
Sammons, P. 12
SATs 92
Schon, D. 48
School Action Plans *see* action plans

155

Index

School Development Plan (SDP) 73, 75, 82–3, 93–4, 95
School Development Service 72, 73, 78, 89
school effectiveness 5–6, 12
School Improvement Literacy Project team 107
School Improvement Officers 137
School Improvement Projects (SIPs) 71, 72, 73–4; case study of productive partnership 75–116; conferences 78, 83–4, 89–90, 97, 104–5, 110; experience of the schools 74; as a force for improvement 77–8; network meetings 78, 83, 90, 110; newsletters 90; process 73
school inspection 28–34; *see also* Office for Standards in Education
school mission statement 15
school performance data 94–5
Scottish CCC 66
Seashore Lewis, K. 137
Self-Assessment Document (SAD) 67
self-assessment profiles 28
self-confidence 122
self-determination 63–4
self-examination 31
self-identity 7
self-review, validated *see* validated self-review
self-review sheets 101
Senge, P.M. 59, 143
shaming 14, 33, 40, 49–50
shared value system 72
sharing 83–4, 97
sharing–learning culture 48
simulations 123
Single Regeneration Budget 89
socio-economic disadvantage 71–2
Sony Walkman 3
Special Needs Support Service 72
spirit of inquiry 70
sponsorship, business 26
stakeholder survey 95, 98, 141
Stalker, G.M. 53
standards 13, 19; conformity to common 40–2; developing new quality standards 35–6; inspection and 28–9; in higher education 56–8
Stiegelbanner, S. 26, 50, 126, 135
strategic approach to quality 30–1
stress tolerance 123
students: as customers 11

study skills 101, 102, 103
subject areas/departments 56, 57, 68
summative assessment 6, 43
supervision 43–4
support, external 141–3; LEA and 89–90, 98–9, 111–13
surveys 119
Synectics process 126–8

targets 4, 37–8; SIP 101, 102, 103–4
task groups 124, 137–8, 142–3
tasks: high-need achievers and 139
teacher-based assessment 6–7
Teacher Training Agency 14
teachers: control of education 16, 17; development review *see* development review; impact of SIPs on skills and expertise 114; and learning 47–8, 59; managing teaching and learning while reacting to outside influences 50, 52
teaching: amount and type undertaken 24; improvement as a complex process 23–6; outcomes 25–6; overall planning of 24–5; quality of in higher education 58; in the 'Quality' school 19–20
teaching standards policy 23
Technical and Vocational Enterprise Initiative (TVEI) 142
Teesdale Primary School 81–6; dissemination and sharing 83–4; evaluation 84–6; refining the school's thinking 83; reviewing curriculum planning 82–3
templates 57
Thompson, D. 30
tight-loose properties 53
time 118, 132; effective time management 132–3
time-related outcomes 38
total quality management (TQM) 3, 34–6
trust 33, 46, 54, 55
Turrell, D. 142
Tysome, T. 56

underachievement 100
United States of America 9, 54–5, 74
universities *see* higher education

validated self-review 33–4, 60–74, 140–3; background to case study 70–4; case

study 75–116; in higher and further education 66–70; local context for quality improvement 72–3; partnership for quality 62–6; and quality development 60–2; School Improvement Projects (SIPs) 73–4
valuations, higher and lower 17
value judgements 14
variation 6
vision 15–16, 120
visionary companies 8

Walkman, Sony 3
Washington, G. 54–5
Waterman, R.H. 1, 53, 137–8

Weick, K. 59
West, M. 115
Whitaker, P. 49
Wideacre Primary School 92–9; evaluation 96–9; gaining commitment 95–6; school improvement 93–5
Wilcox, B. 29, 47
Winch, C. 4
Wood, M. 31, 38, 124
workload 24
worksheets 106
Wragg, T. 33, 50, 134

zero tolerance 14